Introduction

The Battle of Britain Memorial Flight was born on July 11, 1957 with the arrival of three Mk XIX Spitfires at RAF Biggin Hill. From what little I know of our founder, Group Captain Peter Thompson DFC, he would have been pleasantly surprised to know that the BBMF had reached its 60th anniversary, yet modest about the debt we owe him for setting up the Historic Aircraft Flight.

Thompson was a Battle of Britain pilot, one of the fabled 'Few'. His generation, which sadly grows fewer day-by-day, is possessed of amazing stoicism, self-deprecation and a compelling sense of duty and patriotism. They are a generation to whom all of us living in this fine country owe our freedom. They are also a generation from whom we can learn humility, determination, dignity and loyalty.

These qualities are writ large, both in Group Captain Thompson's actions and in the few words of his we have in our records. I'm certain that without his vision and determination we would have no BBMF and no spectacular reminder of the sacrifices that were made for us. We would be a poorer nation for it. Senior officers from air forces around the world routinely visit our base at Royal Air Force Coningsby in Lincolnshire, ostensibly to see the Typhoon, but invariably end up coming to view the Flight's fantastic aircraft. They are unfailingly impressed and not a little jealous that the Royal Air Force has such a jewel in its crown.

Just Getting On With It

That BBMF is in its 60th year is also an acute reminder of the marching of time, the most precious resource any of us possess. Our wonderful surviving veterans continue to visit the Flight, where we laud them and delight in their company. But with time they are finite and I urge you one and all to set about meeting the generation of World War Two. They are charming, selfless and fascinating. They think nothing of what they went through, accepting their lot with a shrug – they were 'just getting on with it'. Find out about them – they love to talk to younger people and tell them of their experiences. We are lucky on the Flight to count many of them as our friends; I hope that you might do the same.

To honour these men, this season we have repainted several of our aircraft in the markings and colours of surviving veterans. Among them, our Mk IIA Spitfire, P7350, is arguably the most precious flying machine on the planet, as the last Spitfire still flying that fought in the Battle of Britain. This year she will bear the markings of two of the remaining Few, Geoff Wellum and Ken Wilkinson. Hurricane LF363 will be marked with Tom Neil and Paul Farnes's code letters. They were both Hurricane pilots in the Battle.

The Lancaster will be painted on its left-hand side in the colours of 460 Squadron, an Australian unit operating from RAF Binbrook. Dave Fellowes, another surviving veteran, was

Top: This year is Sqn Ldr Millikin's second as OC BBMF. Sgt Andy Benson/© UK MoD Crown Copyright 2017

The Flight's five Spitfires include its latest aircraft addition, Mk XVI TE311. SAC Jack Welson/© UK MoD Crown Copyright 2017

Celebration and commemoration are at the core of BBMF's existence. Here Lancaster PA474 drops poppies over London on the occasion of the 50th anniversary of D-Day in 1995. © UK MoD Crown Copyright 2017

Tattershall Castle forms a striking backdrop to BBMF's operations at RAF Coningsby, just as it did to those of 97 Sqn, the second operational Lancaster unit, which began re-equipping at the Lincolnshire station in January 1942. The Flight indeed, seems to have come home. Cpl Phil Major/© UK MoD Crown Copyright 2017

They remind us, through a shared corporate memory, of why Britain is great.

Because of this, we plan to keep these aircraft flying as long as is humanly possible – I believe this should be a national aim. With that in mind, 60 years from now it is my very sincere wish that another of Peter Thompson's lucky successors will be writing the introduction to the Royal Air Force *Salute* celebrating 120 years of the BBMF. I also trust that he or she signs off with the Royal Air Force Battle of Britain Memorial Flight's motto: Lest We Forget. ⊙

Squadron Leader Andy 'Milli' Millikin, Officer Commanding Battle of Britain Memorial Flight

a wartime tail gunner on 460 and remains the Flight's firm friend. The Lancaster's right-hand side will wear 50 Squadron markings for 'VN-T' for 'Tommy'. John Tait, the wireless operator on this aircraft, is the last surviving member of a crew skippered by my grandfather, Doug Millikin.

Best of British

For me, the BBMF's aircraft and the men who flew them represent the very finest characteristics of the British. In their day the aircraft were at the leading edge of technological advancement, a bright shining sword with which the Royal Air Force could fight and often better the enemy. They symbolise innovation, intelligence, grit and vision. They are also, as a happy but unintended consequence, among the most beautiful flying machines ever created. They hark back to a simpler time.

You may consider this is an overly rose-tinted view of Britain's history. Maybe so. But it's one that captures the imagination and stirs the soul. Only a very cold heart could not be moved by the thought of those young men who fought gallantly, often desperately, only to lose their lives serving in the RAF.

There is a magic about these aircraft that, rather like the sight of a thatched pub on a village green in summer, or the white cliffs of Dover, truly symbolises our remarkable nation. That's why the British public love them so.

A relatively small team of engineers works tirelessly to keep BBMF's historic aircraft flying. Deeper winter maintenance is performed under the watchful gaze of myriad visitors, touring the Flight's hangar via the publicly accessible visitor centre located alongside. Cpl Phil Major/© UK MoD Crown Copyright 2017

Aircrew who volunteer for the Flight thrill in the challenge of operating its aircraft, including the Dakota, but all report that the most rewarding part of the job is meeting veterans. © UK MoD Crown Copyright 2017

His Royal Highness The Duke of Cambridge with then OC BBMF Sqn Ldr Dunc Mason, preparing to go flying in a Chipmunk in September 2015.
LAC Jack Welson/© UK MoD Crown Copyright 2017

Foreword

KENSINGTON PALACE

As patron of the Royal Air Force Battle of Britain Memorial Flight it gives me great pleasure to write this foreword on the occasion of the Flight's Sixtieth Anniversary.

There are few sights or sounds that evoke a more emotional response than a display or flypast by the iconic aircraft of the BBMF. They tug at the heart strings, bringing many to tears; they generate a sense of pride, lifting the spirits of veterans and the public alike and they inspire all those who see them. The Flight's aircraft provide a living tribute of the nation's respect for all who those who have served with the Royal Air Force across the generations; especially those who have lost their lives fighting to preserve the freedom of others.

Sixty years on from the Flight's inception in 1957 the BBMF's historic aircraft are maintained and flown to the same exacting standards as the most modern aircraft in the Royal Air Force. The aircrew and engineers operate these aircraft with the same professionalism, dedication and selflessness of those who went before them, in far more dangerous circumstances during World War Two. In those six decades the BBMF has displayed or flown past at thousands of events, including State occasions and major commemorations. The Flight has become a household name and a national institution. With its synthesis of old and modern, then and now, the BBMF represents a continuance of the core values of the Royal Air Force; professional excellence, teamwork and selflessness.

The next time that you see the BBMF aircraft, apart from marvelling at the sheer spectacle and symphonic sound, please recognise the tribute offered to all those who have died serving in the Royal Air Force and, at the same time, spare a thought for those who continue to serve today.

Spitfire Mk VB AB910.
Jim Dooley Photography

Contents

ROYAL AIR FORCE

Published in association with Royal Air Force Media and Communications, Headquarters Air Command

EDITORIAL
Editor: Paul E Eden
Group Editor: Nigel Price

DESIGN
Studio Manager: Steve Donovan
Design: Tracey Croft, Dan Jarman, Dominique Maynard

PRODUCTION
Production Manager:
Janet Watkins

ADVERTISING and MARKETING
Senior Advertisement Manager:
Ian Maxwell
Advertising Group Manager:
Brodie Baxter
Advertising Production Manager:
Debi McGowan
Group Marketing Manager:
Martin Steele
Marketing:
Shaun Binnington, Amy Donkersley, Lillie Elliot

COMMERCIAL DIRECTOR:
Ann Saundry
PUBLISHER and MANAGING DIRECTOR: Adrian Cox
EXECUTIVE CHAIRMAN:
Richard Cox

CONTACTS
Key Publishing Ltd
PO Box 100, Stamford,
Lincolnshire, PE9 1XQ, UK
Tel: 01780 755131
Fax: 01780 757261
E-mail : enquiries@keypublishing.com
www.keypublishing.com

DISTRIBUTION
Seymour Distribution Ltd
2 Poultry Avenue, London EC1A 9PP
020 7429 400

PRINTED BY
Warners (Midlands) plc, The Maltings, Bourne, Lincs PE10 9PH

PUBLISHER
Key Publishing Ltd
PRINTED IN ENGLAND

COVER IMAGE:
Battle of Britain Memorial Flight Hurricane LF363 and Spitfire P7350. John Dibbs Photography

Display performances are designed to entertain and educate, while conserving airframe and engine life. Here AB910 displays back in 2007. Ian Forshaw/© UK MoD Crown Copyright 2017

I'm Flying a Spitfire!

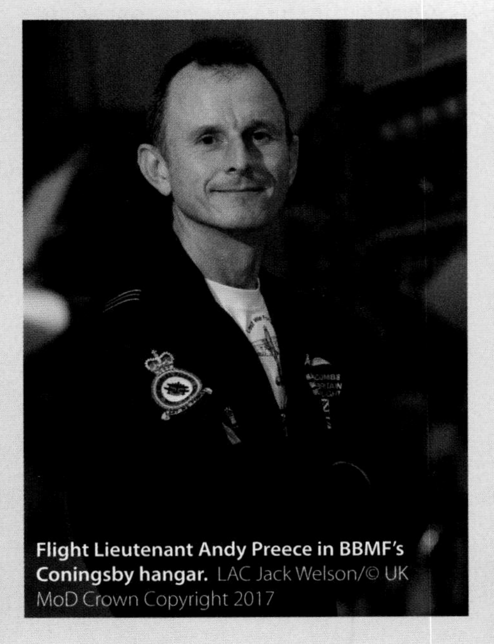

Flight Lieutenant Andy Preece in BBMF's Coningsby hangar. LAC Jack Welson/© UK MoD Crown Copyright 2017

Flight Lieutenant Andy Preece can hardly believe his luck every time he flies a BBMF Spitfire! Here he shares the excitement and exacting work of a typical display routine

At the top of the list of jobs I thought I'd never have, 'Spitfire Display Pilot' sits just below 'Apollo Astronaut'. But in 2016 I got to be just that, a Spitfire display pilot. I don't think I've ever driven to RAF Coningsby, home of the RAF BBMF, without a feeling of disbelief that I'm going there to fly a Spitfire! Of our six Spitfires, each with its own incredible history, I was extremely lucky to fly three last year.

All our aircraft are affectionately referred to as 'ladies' and therefore generally referred to as 'she' in discussion. The Spitfires, especially the 'babies' (Mks II and V) are prone to overheating, so engine start and taxi have to be timed to avoid delays in getting airborne; once the aircraft's aloft it receives maximum airflow through its radiator.

Flying a Spitfire is always the same for me. As take-off time is reached, the adrenaline is in full flow as I watch the seconds down to zero on my watch. I carefully advance the throttle forward towards take-off power. It seems to move a long way and, despite the incredible noise, only when I look at the boost gauge do I realise just how far. The gauge essentially gives me an idea of how much output the supercharger is producing. Since engine rpm is set separately, power changes are achieved by reference to the boost gauge (it's a little like manifold pressure on general aviation aircraft with variable-pitch propellers).

So I keep pushing the throttle forwards, keeping her straight, and ease the control column gently forwards to lift the tail. With my right leg I push increasingly hard on the rudder pedal as various adverse forces combine to urge her into a dart for the side of the runway. Easing back on the control column, we're off! I immediately need to swap hands so I can retract the undercarriage (the lever is on the right-hand side and my right hand is on the control column), close the canopy and reduce the rpm setting to look after the engine. I'm flying a Spitfire!

... You Are Cleared Display

Typically we fly several flypasts on the way to a display, and since limiting airborne time is a priority, we tend to fly in straight lines between events, leaving little time to relax. We have various options for the display: single aircraft, multiple fighters and, of course, our signature display with the Lancaster and Hurricane, although the typical Spitfire display actually remains unchanged as part of a mixed display.

Arriving at the site, I go through my pre-display checks and then start positioning for my run-in. "Spitfire 96, you are cleared »

display, QFE 1010." "Cleared display, 1010 set, Spitfire 96." I'm cleared to display and '1010' refers to the setting I must have on my altimeter to give me a height reference above the display site.

Now I make sure the throttle friction is fully tight – think of it as a clamp without which the throttle would sneak back towards a lower power setting due to vibration, with a result something like taking your foot of the accelerator in a car; it's not what you want halfway through a display!

I position the aircraft for a run-in on the 'B' axis at around 2,000ft. It's an imaginary line running out from the centre of the display line at 90° to the crowd. I'll have studied the 'B' axis position before flight, either on an Ordnance Survey map or satellite photograph and chosen an object along it for reference. I turn onto it, allowing a little for my turn radius, then point either left or right of the display centre or 'datum', compensating for the wind and thus tracking the line.

Into a gentle dive and it starts to get noisy in the cockpit, although nowhere near as noisy as in the Hurricane. I trim the aircraft, making sure she's in balance – it's something I'll need to repeat every time the speed changes. I arrive at crowd centre at around 270kt, approximately 310mph, and down at my minimum altitude of 100ft.

I need to judge where to start my turn. The closest I'm allowed to the crowd is 230m and although the line is normally physically marked on the ground, I picture a wall, between them and me; any closer and the display director will call me to stop. As I start the turn I'm hoping the crowd is savouring the iconic sound of the Merlin purring away at display power setting – the maximum power we use during BBMF Merlin fighter operations is 7psi boost, roughly half of what the engine can produce. If there's any downside to flying these beautiful machines, it's that you don't get to enjoy that amazing sound from the inside!

Going into the turn, my aim is to apex just on my side of the 230m line, then roll out going away from the crowd at 30°, showing off the classic elliptical wing shape as I do. Each line of the display is adjusted by plus or minus a few seconds as appropriate for the wind of the day, and I might aim left or right of each line to prevent drift. I also try to pick something in the distance as an aiming point, flying out on the crowd-right, 30° line for a few seconds, then pulling up into a Derry wingover.

This manoeuvre consists of a pull-up to about 30° nose high, then a roll 'in the wrong direction'; if I want to end up in a right hand turn, I initially roll left and go all the way under until I end up at about 60° angle of bank to the right. The result is a graceful manoeuvre that enables me to perform a fairly tight turn while gaining height and therefore energy that I can use in my next manoeuvre.

The Spitfire Mk V shows off the type's classic elliptical wing shape. Andy Preece's previous display mount, the Grob Tutor, at left, was dramatically less powerful than the Spitfire, but nonetheless required precision flying from its pilot. Cpl Neil Condie & Gordon Elias/© UK MoD Crown Copyright 2017

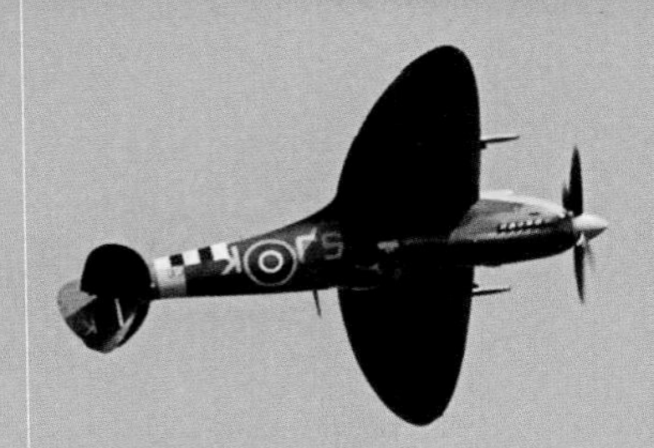

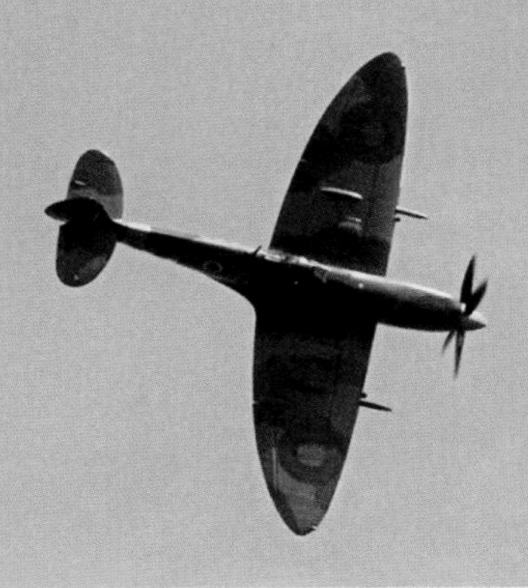

This image sequence shows the victory roll that completes the Spitfire display. Clive Rowley

The Spitfire rolls beautifully. In fact the roll rate of the clipped-wing Mk XVI is comparable to that of a modern aircraft. I have to be extremely careful when pulling up into the Derry wingover not to exceed the maximum 3.5*g* limit on the aircraft. As with everything else we do, the emphasis is on mechanical empathy and conservation – we would like BBMF to be flying in another 60 years and so we fly to limits well below those of the design capability.

Having converted my speed to height in the turn, I position for the high-speed pass, a run down the display line at 100ft and our maximum display speed of 270kt. The Spitfire is capable of flying much faster, but with our limited power settings and airframe longevity in mind, we limit it to 270kt. Flying along the display line and past display datum I have my first real chance for a good look at the crowd – I can see individuals as I fly past, so I'll know if you're watching or not!

It doesn't take long to reach the other end, and a few seconds after passing datum it's time to pull up into another Derry wingover, again to the left and finishing in a right-hand turn. I watch the *g* and then check the engine instruments, because the engine has to be monitored for irregularities throughout the display.

Coming back towards datum, the next manoeuvre is the Orbit, a 360° turn with the aircraft flying higher at the 'back' of the circle. I have to think about the wind here and make subtle adjustments to my turn rate to achieve what looks like an equally spaced circle to the crowd. If I fly it correctly, the aircraft should appear level at the halfway point, but higher than when I started. If I flew a level turn, the crowd wouldn't be able to see the Spitfire when I was further away.

Finishing the turn on the crowd-right 30° line, it's time for another Derry wingover. You might be thinking this all sounds a bit samey? It may actually be a fair point, but the display is purposely kept that way for many reasons. We avoid a complicated display so that the sequence is relatively easy to learn and pilots require only minimum hours on the aircraft to become proficient. It also means that a pilot doesn't require so many hours of currency to remain practiced. The format is designed to demonstrate the aircraft's beauty, not the pilot's skill – she is the star of the show, not me! It's a graceful display that enables spectators to enjoy the sound and classic lines of the Spitfire, while placing minimal stress on the airframe and engine.

Coming back around onto the display line for another low pass, it's time for the manoeuvre we call the Horseshoe. Just after datum, I roll into a turn that takes me back away from the crowd at 90°. Hopefully I can still see the feature I overflew at the start, because I'll aim to apex there. Aiming left or right to allow for the wind, I pull up and fly »

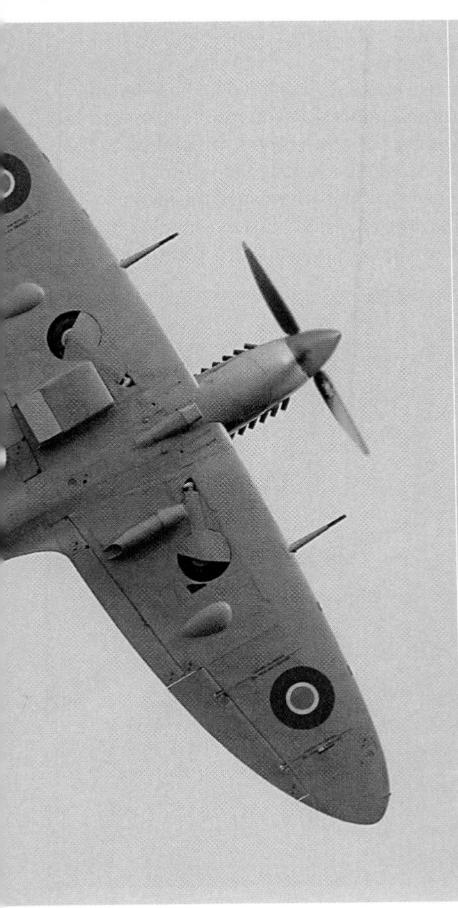

"Displaying the aircraft takes the dream to another level."

MK356 during an evening practice sortie over Coningsby in 2014. Paul E Eden

The BBMF's trademark formation places a fighter on each of the Lancaster's wing tips. Here the Spitfire Mk IX is to port, with Hurricane PZ865 opposite. LA (Phot) Gaz Armes/© UK MoD Crown Copyright 2017

"I can see individuals as I fly past, so I'll know if you're watching or not!"

the shape of an upturned horseshoe, coming out of the manoeuvre back towards the crowd. At the top of the Horseshoe I transmit: "Spitfire, 1 minute." If the Hurricane's following me in it gives him a heads-up that I have a minute left of my display before he takes the stage.

Turning back out to the crowd-left 30° line, again watching the *g*, I pull up into a final Derry wingover, this time in the other direction, calling: "Spitfire, 30 seconds." "Hurricane, Roger." Flying down the display line for the final time, I pull up just before datum to perform the classic victory roll. If I get it right, I should be inverted as I reach datum for the last time and if it's a joint display, I should see the Hurricane at the beginning of her run in. As I pass the end of the display line I take the Spitfire to crowd rear, climb to around 2,000-3,000ft and let her cool down before landing, joining the Lancaster or another fighter, or departing for the next event.

Tutor

I previously spent four seasons displaying the RAF's Elementary Flying Training aircraft, the Grob Tutor. It has a 180hp, four-cylinder Lycoming engine, while the Spitfire's I've flown have a 27-litre V12 Merlin producing more than 1,300hp. The Tutor display comprised a more complex sequence in a fully aerobatic routine and could be very difficult to position in strong winds, which affect the Tutor much more owing to its lower speed and clearance to fly in stronger winds.

But in terms of pure flying, the Spitfire is a far more demanding aircraft, especially during take-off and landing. Additionally of course, the Tutor has modern flight instruments and navigation aids, while the Spitfire is pretty much as it would have been during World War Two and transiting around the country is a real challenge. Displaying the Tutor was a great experience that helped give me the ideal skill set and discipline for displaying the Spitfire.

I guess most pilots dream of flying a Spitfire. Displaying the aircraft takes the dream to another level. It's truly an honour and the ultimate privilege to be entrusted to fly these wonderful machines at airshows and a multitude of other events throughout the UK.

I've just flown a Spitfire!

It's when I've completed the shutdown checks that I'm hit every time with the realisation that I've just been flying a Spitfire. It's partly a feeling of relief – I haven't broken it! Ours are among the most precious and valuable aircraft on the planet and the real heroes of BBMF are those behind the scenes, the dedicated team of engineers and support staff without whom we wouldn't be able to keep these wonderful aircraft flying.

I also imagine how it would have felt in wartime, landing for a quick refuel, re-arm and take-off for another round, remembering that many Spitfire pilots failed to return.

Driving home afterwards, the idea of displaying a Spitfire is just as unreal as it was on the way in. "I've just flown a Spitfire!" ⊙

Spitfire Mk XVI TE311 demonstrates Andy Preece's typical working environment. SAC Daniel Herrick/ © UK MoD Crown Copyright 2017

Spitfire Mk IIA P7350

Squadron Leader Clive Rowley MBE RAF (Retd) tells the story of BBMF's Spitfire Mk IIA

Spitfire Mk IIA P7350, known on the Flight as 'P7', was the 14th of 11,939 Spitfires built at Supermarine's Castle Bromwich 'Shadow' factory, although it was not, in fact, the 14th delivered to the RAF. First flown by the company's famous production test pilot Alex Henshaw in August 1940, it was taken on RAF charge on August 13. Henshaw delivered it to No. 6 Maintenance Unit (MU) at Brize Norton four days later, for the installation of operational equipment.

During the late 1960s and into the 1970s, P7 wore 'ZH-T' codes for 266 Sqn, one of its wartime units. Unfortunately, the squadron only introduced 'ZH' codes on its Typhoons in 1942; its Spitfires had worn 'UO' codes. Key Collection

In this April 2010 photograph, P7 is marked as 92 Sqn's 'QJ-K'. SAC Neil Chapman/© UK MoD Crown Copyright 2017

Squadrons Then and Now

Number	Established	Initial Aircraft	Spitfire Service	2017 Role	Aircraft
603	October 14, 1925	DH.9A	Mk I August 1939-November 1940, Mk IIA November 1940-May 1941, Mk VA May-November 1941, Mk VB August 1941-March 1942, Mk XVI January-August 1945 & June 1946-1947, Mk 22 1947-51	Recruiting and training RAF Police & Regiment Reservists	None

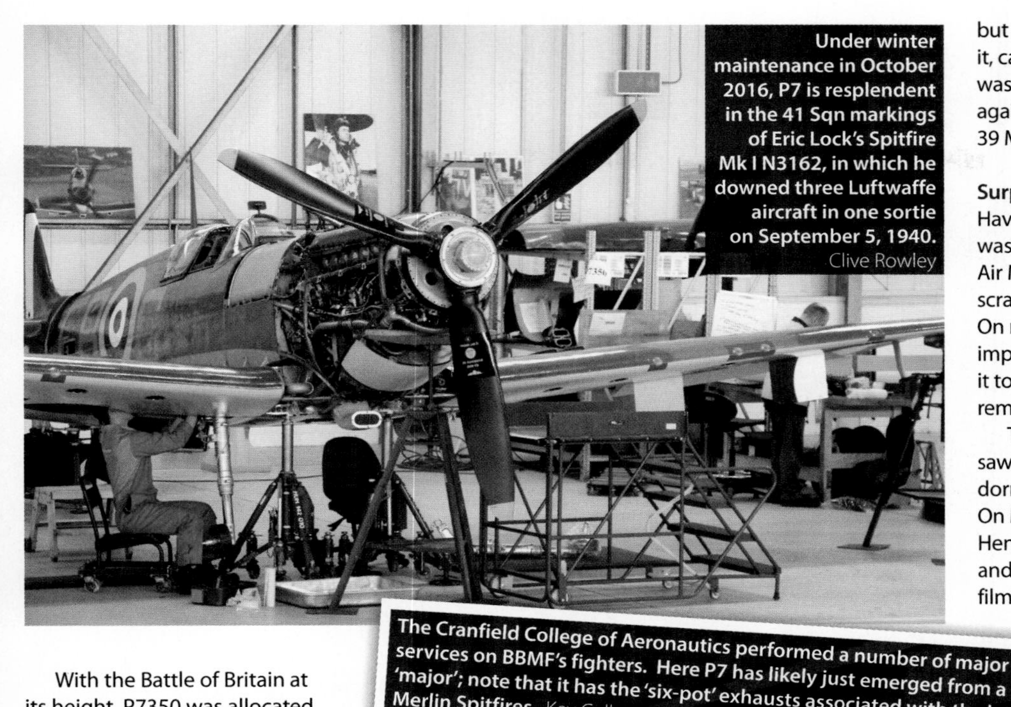

Under winter maintenance in October 2016, P7 is resplendent in the 41 Sqn markings of Eric Lock's Spitfire Mk I N3162, in which he downed three Luftwaffe aircraft in one sortie on September 5, 1940. Clive Rowley

The Cranfield College of Aeronautics performed a number of major services on BBMF's fighters. Here P7 has likely just emerged from a 'major'; note that it has the 'six-pot' exhausts associated with the later Merlin Spitfires. Key Collection

With the Battle of Britain at its height, P7350 was allocated to 266 Sqn at Wittering on September 6, 1940 and given the code letters 'UO-T'. Subsequently, 266 Sqn moved to Martlesham Heath and then Collyweston.

On October 17, P7350 was among 13 Mk IIA Spitfires transferred to 603 (City of Edinburgh) Sqn, Auxiliary Air Force (AuxAF) at Hornchurch. The aircraft's code letters were changed to those of its new unit, and although there is some doubt over P7's individual letter, the best guess is that it wore 'XT-W'.

Down But Not Out

With Polish pilot Ludwik Martel at its controls, on October 25, P7350 fell to a Messerschmitt Bf 109. A cannon shell punched a large hole in its port wing and shrapnel wounded Martel in the left side of his body and legs. In pain, and fighting to remain conscious, Martel flew the aircraft down through 16,000ft of thick cloud before force landing in a field near Hastings.

The aircraft was recovered and dispatched to No. 1 Civilian Repair Unit at Cowley on October 31 for repair. On December 7 it was ready for collection and flown to 37 MU at Burtonwood, Lancashire, for service preparation and storage.

Fighter Sweeps

The aircraft was next operational with 616 (County of South Yorkshire) Sqn, AuxAF at Tangmere, to which it was issued on March 18, 1941. On April 10 it was transferred to 64 Sqn at Hornchurch and with these units, P7350 flew fighter sweeps over occupied Europe as Fighter Command continued on the offensive during 1941.

Later, having apparently incurred damage from an unknown incident, possibly a landing accident, in August 1941 P7350 was moved to Scottish Aviation at Prestwick for overhaul and repair. It was flown to 37 MU again on January 29, 1942.

With higher performance, better-armed versions of the Spitfire now available, the time had come to withdraw the Mk II from operational flying. On April 27, therefore, P7350 was issued to the Central Gunnery School at Sutton Bridge, near King's Lynn. Here it spent the next ten months, suffering a Category B accident (beyond repair on site) on February 4, 1943 and being transferred to Air Services Training at Hamble for repairs.

The work had been completed by March 20, and after passing through 6 MU at Brize Norton again, P7 was issued to 57 Operational Training Unit (OTU) at Eshott, Northumberland. It passed 12 uneventful months as a training machine, but on April 22, 1944 another Spitfire taxied into it, causing further Category B damage; again it was off to Air Services Training for repairs. Once again back in order, P7 was placed in storage at 39 MU, Colerne.

Surplus Spitfire

Having survived its wartime adventures, P7350 was declared surplus to requirements by the Air Ministry in 1947. In 1948, it was sold as scrap to Messrs John Dale and Sons, for £25. On realising the venerable aircraft's historical importance, the company generously presented it to RAF Colerne as a museum piece, where it remained until 1967.

The making of the movie *Battle of Britain* saw Spitfire P7350 emerge from 20 years of dormancy when it was selected for a flying role. On March 3, 1967 it was delivered to 71 MU at Henlow for overhaul to airworthy condition and on May 20, 1968 it was flown to Duxford for filming. With the production complete, P7350 was allocated to the Battle of Britain Flight, Squadron Leader Tim Mills delivering it to the Flight's Coltishall base on November 5, 1968.

2017 Scheme

For the 2017 display season, P7 will wear code letters honouring two surviving members of the Few. The new letters are being applied in a special temporary paint that will cover the existing markings but is easily removed when required.

On the starboard (right-hand) side, the code letters 'QV-E' are those of a 19 Sqn Spitfire flown from Fowlmere by then Sergeant Ken Wilkinson. He joined the unit on October 17, 1940, just two weeks before the Battle of Britain officially ended, having previously served for two weeks with 616 Sqn at Kirton-in-Lindsey, Lincolnshire. Ken was eventually commissioned and reached the rank of Flying Officer.

The code letters 'QJ-G' on P7350's port (left-hand) side are those of the 92 Sqn aircraft flown by Geoffrey Wellum – "G- for Geoffrey," he says; 'QJ-G' replaced his first aircraft, 'QJ-K'. Aged just 19 when he first went into combat in September 1940, Geoffrey was among the youngest pilots in the Battle of Britain. He was officially credited with three enemy aircraft destroyed, four 'probables' and several damaged. He was awarded the DFC in July 1941 and eventually retired from the RAF as a squadron leader.

Wellum once said: "If you remember one of us, then you must remember all of us." ⊙

"If you remember one of us, then you must remember all of us."

Squadron Leader Geoffrey Wellum DFC RAF (Retd)

Fine display items in their own right, the Lancaster and Dakota complement one another perfectly in the BBMF line up. As Bomber Leader, 'Twigs' Dunlop makes careful use of the Dak as a 'trainer' during the Lancaster work-up.
Photo © John Dibbs

Bomber Leader

The Bomber Leader's is a vital role, with responsibility to OC BBMF for the training and rostering of the Lancaster and Dakota aircrew, and for conducting air tests on those aircraft. Flight Lieutenant Tim 'Twigs' Dunlop, the current Bomber Leader, provides a personal insight into the job

Tim Dunlop became Bomber Leader for the 2014 season. SAC Steve Buckley/© UK MoD Crown Copyright 2017

On May 16, 1993, I'd driven to the Derwent Dam with my father and a few of his friends; it's the first time I can remember going somewhere specifically to see the BBMF's Lancaster. We found a spot about 500m up the hill on the western side of the dam and after a few hours' wait she arrived, looking glorious in the afternoon sunshine and sounding amazing. Back then I could only a dream of one day having the honour of flying one of the world's two remaining airworthy Lancasters. Sixteen years later, that dream became reality.

If I'm honest, I joined the RAF with the aspiration of becoming a fast jet pilot. I wanted to fly Tornados. I remember being told that it was not to be, but it turned out to be a lucky turn of fate – had I forged my career in the fast jet fleet I would not have ended up flying the Lancaster. That honour belongs only to a lucky few members of the RAF's multi-engine cadre.

As a student pilot learning to fly multi-engine aircraft with 45(R) Sqn, my primary instructor, Flight Lieutenant Merv Counter, and the Standards Instructor, Squadron Leader David Thomas, were both BBMF Lancaster pilots.

As well as instructing on the Jetstream, they would disappear over to RAF Coningsby and fly the 'Lanc'. I was immensely envious of them, while also being proud that they taught me how to fly.

On completion of my flying training, I was awarded my wings and posted to RAF Lyneham on the C-130K Hercules. I completed a tour as co-pilot and another as captain, before being selected to become a Qualified Flying Instructor (QFI) at RAF Cranwell. Perhaps here was an opportunity to apply to BBMF? I was initially posted to instruct on the Grob Tutor, but because you need to be a current multi-engine pilot to fly the 'heavies' with the BBMF, I requested a posting to 45(R) Sqn.

BBMF Selection

Having successfully negotiated the move to 45(R), which by now had relinquished its Jetstreams for the modern King Air, I was much better placed to have a shot at becoming a Lancaster pilot. After a tough interview with then OC BBMF, Sqn Ldr Al Pinner, I was selected onto the team in 2009.

When I joined the BBMF, the Bomber Leader was Sqn Ldr Stu Reid. First he taught

Twigs's first trip as Lancaster captain, August 19, 2011.

"I try to give everyone roughly the same number of hours – I wouldn't want a revolt on my hands!"

On May 16, 1993, Tim Dunlop watched PA474 overfly the Derwent Dam on the 50th anniversary of the Dam Busters' raid. Twenty years later, he flew the aircraft over the same spot to mark the raid's 70th. Chief Tech John Christian/© UK MoD Crown Copyright 2017

me how to fly the Dakota. New pilots usually spend roughly half the first season flying only the 'Dak', building their multi-engine 'tail-dragger' experience before advancing to co-pilot on the Lancaster. After a couple of years on the team, pilots may be selected to become Lancaster captains.

I vividly remember my first flight as a trainee Lancaster captain in the left seat. Taxying out at Bournemouth Airport on August 19, 2011, I was quite nervous under the instruction of Flt Lt Ernie Taylor. It was a surreal experience, sitting in the long-coveted seat. I had studied hard to ensure I was as prepared as I could be, but as co-pilot you don't handle the Lancaster on take-off or landing.

I remember her yawing slightly to the left as we accelerated down the runway, just as Ernie had briefed me she would; the forward push on the control column needed to bring the tail up was much greater than I had expected and then, after a pull back, she was flying. The airborne elements were as I had expected; I had handled her many times away from the ground as co-pilot from the other seat. Soon it was time to return to Bournemouth and as I lined up with the runway, I took a sharp intake of breath and attempted my first ever Lancaster landing.

Twigs displays the Dakota as well as the Lancaster. Cpl Paul Robertshaw/© UK MoD Crown Copyright 2017

Fast-forward a couple of years to September 2013 and I was walking through St Andrews with then OC BBMF, Sqn Ldr Dunc Mason. He was discussing who would be the next Bomber Leader – I suggested a couple of names before he asked me if I fancied the job. Honoured isn't the word! I had already become a Dakota QFI and more recently a Lancaster QFI, now it was time to take on the dream job!

I took over as Bomber Leader in October 2013. As it turned out, 2014, my first full year in the role, was the year of the famous Two Lancasters Tour – it was an exciting time!

Living The Dream

The RAF refers to my BBMF role as 'secondary duty', meaning that I have a primary duty elsewhere – in my case that's flying the A400M Atlas. Most RAF officers have a secondary duty. It might be serving as secretary on a committee, organising annual balls or running charity funds. Mine is flying a Dakota and a Lancaster – not bad at all!

For us part-time BBMF volunteer aircrew, the primary job takes priority during the winter months, as we attempt to get back into our Boss' good books! There's no doubt that BBMF duties take a toll on the frontline RAF squadrons that loan aircrew. It's our colleagues on the squadrons who often take up the slack while we're not there, and thanks must go to all those who help us fulfil the BBMF commitment. The winter provides me the opportunity to give something back.

Alongside flying the Atlas, I also review all the BBMF 'Bomber' documentation and ensure we're ready for the start of the next display season. Come January, I review all the teaching notes and work out the details for the training days, one for the Dakota and, later, one for the Lancaster.

Pre-season

The training days are usually held in February, as an essential part of the pre-season work-up. Each year I invite various members of the Bomber cadre to brief a technical aspect of »

Flt Lt Dunlop with Canadian Warplane Heritage Museum Lancaster pilot Don Schofield, in 2014. © UK MoD Crown Copyright 2017

the aircraft or a procedure, such as the display or a visual circuit. Allocating crewmembers different aspects to brief means they have to research the subject, giving them, and everyone else a better understanding. Working with the Navigator, Flight Engineer and Loadmaster Leaders, I ensure the days are of maximum benefit.

By March the aircrew begin to get excited! The engineers have worked extremely hard over the winter maintenance period and it's time to fly the aircraft again. I write a work-up programme that fits around everyone's primary jobs, while ensuring we'll be ready to display under the watchful eye of Air Officer Commanding 1 Group on Public Display Approval (PDA) day. I'm usually teased about the number of amendments that are made due to weather or other unforeseen delays…

Dakota

The first trip of the year for me is an air test in the Dakota; it's a thorough shakedown of the aircraft and her systems to check she's ready for the season ahead. Of course, there's no simulator to practise in beforehand, so I spend a lot of time studying my notes and reminding myself how to fly her. After the air test I take a further training sortie to hone my own skill set before beginning the process of training everyone else.

The first people taught are the other instructors, not just the other QFI, but the navigator and loadmaster instructors too. The training routine changes subtly each year depending on how many new team members there are – new members get a few more hours.

Lancaster

With everyone comfortable in the Dakota, the Lancaster air test is flown. By now I've usually built between 15 and 20 hours on the Dakota while training everyone else, but the first flight on PA474 is still very daunting. I spend hours studying and find myself taking quite a few moments of quiet contemplation beforehand.

I'm always relieved when the first Lancaster landing of the year is behind me. A misjudged landing results in a series of bounces down the runway, which can damage the aircraft; there's also the potential for a 'ground-loop' (tail-draggers can easily swap direction on the runway, turning through 180° if they're not watched carefully).

After the air test, a programme of work-up training, similar to that for the Dakota, is completed. When we're all comfortable with flying the aircraft we polish the display routines; I'll often be found in the air traffic control tower reviewing pilots' routines so that we're ready for PDA.

The number of training sorties on the Lancaster and Dakota is the result of a carefully considered balance, since we have only a set number of flying hours each year. Too much training reduces the number of events we can attend, while too few hours won't allow for the high standard expected of BBMF.

Display Ready

As the work-up progresses, the team begins learning the year's venues. I write a programme for the pilots, while the other section leaders create their own rosters. We're not allowed to fly junior members together and first-year pilots are not permitted to display at certain venues owing to terrain or other complications. In addition, new pilots have a more restrictive minimum landing distance and lower crosswind limits, and all these restrictions need to be considered.

The programmes also depend on primary frontline tasking, and individual preferences for particular venues. To ensure fairness, I try to give everyone roughly the same number of hours – I wouldn't want a revolt on my hands!

Once PDA is over I can relax a little. The work-up is certainly the busiest time of year and I'm always relieved when we're finally allowed to wear our black flying suits again. The display season always throws up challenges as frontline operations change people's availability or the aircraft have technical problems. I plan at least one flying training day every month so we can all get together, but it also ensures that a high standard of flying is maintained. In addition, of course, I have my own share of flying and displaying in the Lancaster and Dakota.

This year is my ninth with the team and I'm already training my successor, although I've a few years left before it's his turn as Bomber Leader. The role's a huge privilege and I know I'm making very special memories. I meet some amazing veterans and it's an honour to represent them every time we take these beautiful aircraft into the air. ⊙

Primary duty – flying the Atlas airlifter with CXX Sqn.

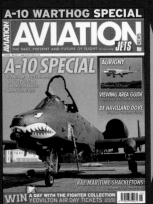

The Air Ministry designated the C-47A as the Dakota Mk III for RAF service. FD903 posed for this image in July 1943. Key Collection

Dakota Defined

These 233 Sqn Dakotas were lined up on the perimeter track at Blakehill Farm, Wiltshire, ready for an exercise with the 6th Airborne Division on April 20, 1944. Very similar scenes preceded the D-Day operation on June 6. RAF (AHB)/© UK MoD Crown Copyright 2017

BBMF's Dakota taxiies in after a Public Display Authority sortie in spring 2016. Cpl Phil Major/© UK MoD Crown Copyright 2017

Easily overlooked in their apparently mundane transport role, the Douglas Dakota and Skytrain series fought in almost every theatre of World War Two, playing key parts in many of the conflict's most important battles. Paul E Eden revisits the Dakota story

In March 1943, No. 24 Sqn began using the Douglas Dakota Mk I on regular communications sorties between Britain and Gibraltar. The type's arrival marked a turning point in Royal Air Force transport operations, moving the service away from the modified bombers, bomber-transports, essentially civilian designs, impressed airliners and light aircraft that formed the majority of its motley transport fleet.

The Dakota Mk I was essentially identical to the C-47 Skytrain, an aircraft already widespread among the US Army Air Force's transport units, having entered service in January 1942. The C-47's origins lay in the DC-3 airliner, first flown on December 18, 1935 and widely considered to have heralded the modern age of airline flying. It offered fine performance and exceptional safety for the era, featured retractable undercarriage and a spacious cabin that acknowledged the requirement for passenger comfort, and quickly proved itself in service with many of the world's airlines.

Militarised through the addition of a reinforced floor, large port side cargo door, basic crew seating, glider-towing gear and other essential equipment, the DC-3 became the rugged C-47, capable of taking the majority of military kit almost anywhere. The RAF named the type Dakota and took 1,900 through the Lend-Lease programme.

Powered by Pratt & Whitney R-1830-92 Twin Wasp radial piston engines, the Dakota Mk I was equivalent to the C-47, while the Mk II was similar to the C-53 Skytrooper, a dedicated troop transport that had entered USAAF service in October 1941. The Dakota Mk III matched the C-47A with an improved electrical system, while the Mk IV was a C-47B equivalent, fitted with supercharged R-1830-90 engines.

Dakotas and Skytrains proved essential to Allied operations in every theatre during the latter half of the war, particularly the airborne assaults on D-Day and subsequently at Arnhem, during the especially difficult campaign in Burma and the final crossing of the Rhine into Germany's heart. The initial three RAF Dakota operators nicely reflect the type's broad geographical spread, 24 Sqn operating from Britain, while 31 Sqn began operations over Burma in March 1943 and 117 Sqn took the aircraft into service in the Middle East during June. »

Squadrons Then and Now

Number	Established	Initial Aircraft	Dakota Service	2017 Role	Aircraft
24 (XXIV)	September 21, 1915	DH.2 (from February 1916)	Mk I, March-August 1943; Mk III February 1944-45; Mk IV 1944-50	Air Mobility operational conversion	Atlas, C-17, Hercules
31	October 1915	B.E.2c	Mk I March 1943-1944; Mk III May 1943-1945; Mk IV February 1945-September 1946 and November 1946-December 1947	Offensive Support	Tornado

Dak Operations

On D-Day, June 6, 1944, Dakotas dropped the majority of the 3rd Parachute Brigade over Normandy and towed Horsa gliders loaded with troops and equipment, releasing them to glide down for controlled crash landings in French fields. In September, the Dakota returned to European skies in force, once again delivering paratroops and gliders into battle, this time in an attempt to establish a stronghold at Arnhem on the Dutch/German border. The Dakota's role was within Operation Market, the airborne complement to ground movements under Operation Garden, but history records the combined operation as a costly failure.

Nonetheless, the larger part of the Allied advance was unstoppable and on March 24, 1945, the Allies launched Operation Varsity, using a massive force of transport aircraft, including hundreds of Dakotas and C-47s, in an airborne assault across the Rhine. The attack marked the beginning of the final push towards Berlin.

Such was the Dakota's versatility though, that it continued as a vital post-war RAF asset. Somewhat ironically, its next major operation was the 1948/49 Berlin Airlift, a mammoth effort during which the West demonstrated its determination to feed the people of West Berlin after Soviet forces cut supply routes into the city. And it was back to war in 1956, when Dakotas engaged in psychological operations against terrorists in the Malayan jungle. The type continued in small scale service overseas until 1966 and finally faded from regular operations on April 1, 1970.

Photographed in September 1944, this Dakota Mk IV has glider towing equipment in its tailcone. Key Collection

With a long and fascinating history behind it, the Battle of Britain Memorial Flight's Dakota C.Mk 3 (Mk III prior to 1948) now appears as a popular display item in its own right. But it also fulfils a role that would be totally familiar to crews 75 years ago, moving the Flight's engineering personnel, kit and supplies around the country when it detaches aircraft away from Coningsby during the display season, serving faithfully and with little drama, as the Dakota always has.

ZA947, the Flight's Dakota C3, is marked with the black and white stripes applied to aircraft involved in the D-Day assault and operations in its immediate aftermath. SAC Graham Taylor/© UK MoD Crown Copyright 2017

Specially modified Lancasters dropped the Upkeep mines employed in the May 1943 Dams raid. All Key Collection unless otherwise stated

Lancaster Legend

An aircraft of epic reputation, the Lancaster quickly evolved into the most capable RAF bomber of World War Two and arguably ranks among the finest combat aircraft ever created

Among PA474's many BBMF identities, *PHANTOM OF THE RUHR* represented Lancaster B.Mk III EE139, a 100 Sqn aircraft that accumulated 121 missions.

If the Hurricane took existing technologies to their limits and the Spitfire heralded a new era in fighter design and construction, then the Lancaster emerged from an appalling engine/airframe combination through relatively simple alterations. The Avro Manchester's twin Rolls-Royce Vulture powerplant suffered chronic unreliability which, combined with control issues, poor crew provision and other issues, created a bomber that was pushed out to operational squadrons from November 1940 for the capability it promised, rather than the performance it delivered.

Recognising the limitations of the 24-cylinder, 'X'-type Vulture, in 1939 Avro began work on a four-engined version, powered by the exemplary Merlin. By the beginning of 1940 the work was near complete, but the urgency with which Merlins were required for the Hurricane and Spitfire saw the Air Ministry press on with Manchester production in hopes the aircraft's problems might be ironed out in service.

By August it had become clear that four-engined heavy bombers would indeed be the means by which the war was taken back to Germany and on the 28th, the Air Ministry announced its intention to prioritise four-engined bomber development. Accordingly, Avro was requested to complete the 700 Manchesters on order, before switching to production of the Handley Page Halifax. It was a request at which Avro's senior management baulked. Not only did they consider their four-engined 'heavy' the better aircraft, but the Manchester production lines could be reconfigured for the new aircraft without the need for complete retooling. The Air Ministry agreed and on September 7 ordered a prototype, for delivery within four months.

Manchester III

Initially known as the Manchester Mk III but quickly rechristened Lancaster, the four-engined bomber featured extended outer wings mounting the additional engine pair and the triple fin and undercarriage arrangements of the original Manchester. It employed the Merlin X around which Avro's original four-engined concept had been designed, but Merlin XX engines were specified for production machines.

Modified from a Manchester, the Lancaster prototype flew for the first time on January 9, 1941. Acceptance trials began at Boscombe Down on the 27th and even with its suboptimal powerplant, the aircraft impressed its pilots. The second prototype took its maiden flight on May 13. Unlike the first it included full defensive armament, along with Merlin XXs, a modified undercarriage with larger wheels and the twin-fin empennage of the later Manchesters. »

PA474 as the centrepiece of the classic three-ship BBMF formation, with Spitfire VB AB910 and Hurricane IIC LF363. Sgt Jack Pritchard/© UK MoD Crown Copyright 2017

Delivered to Boscombe on August 16, it soon began revealing the Lancaster's potential.

Avro's chief designer, Roy Chadwick had remained faithful to Air Ministry requirements when he created the Manchester, although he was sceptical of the official engine choice throughout. Of particular relevance to the Lancaster was the original requirement: "That alternative range performance and bomb load combinations should be exploitable without modification to the airframe, fuel tankage or bomb bay." The offensive load envisaged included at least 8,000lb of bombs, with a pair of 18in torpedoes as an alternative. In making this possible, Chadwick designed a massive, uninterrupted bomb bay that occupied much of the fuselage underside.

When the Manchester morphed into the Lancaster, this unprecedented capacity for bomb carriage was retained; the 4,000lb High Capacity (HC) bomb was easily accommodated, yet it was the largest weapon available to the Halifax. The Lancaster went on to carry 8,000lb and 12,000lb HC bombs (created by joining 4,000lb units), as well as the 12,000lb Tallboy and 22,000lb Grand Slam deep penetration bombs, and it will always be associated with Barnes Wallis's 9,500lb Upkeep mine, the so-called 'bouncing bomb' used by 617 Sqn in the famous Dambusters raid of May 1943.

Main Force & Set Pieces

The first frontline Lancaster unit, No. 44 Sqn began replacing its Handley Page Hampdens with the type in December 1941. It had been flying service trials with the first prototype at its Waddington base since September and after the initial production Lancaster completed its maiden flight on October 31, re-equipment began in earnest. From January 1942, No. 97 Sqn at Coningsby also began the conversion process and on March 3, No. 44 Sqn flew the first of 156,000 Lancaster combat sorties, minelaying in the Heligoland Bight. The first Lancaster bombing mission saw two 44 Sqn aircraft join a raid against Essen on the night of March 10/11.

By April, 44 and 97 Sqns had amassed sufficient aircraft, crews and expertise to mount the first of the Lancaster's headline-grabbing set-piece raids. Debate continues over the true effectiveness of these operations, which typically tasked a relatively small force against a precision target, exemplified by the April 17, 1942 attack on the MAN diesel engine works at Augsburg.

A combined force of 12 Lancasters launched for the low-level daylight strike, suffering heavily under fighter attack and from ground fire. Seven aircraft were lost, although production at the plant was interrupted. Squadron Leader John Nettleton led the raid and received the Victoria Cross for his courage and leadership.

Less obviously, on August 18/19, Lancasters flew with the Pathfinder Force (PFF) for the first time, while the type returned to headline making with the combined 49 and 57 Sqn raid on the Le Creusot weapons factories on October 17. The Dams raid followed on May 17, 1943, flown by 617 Sqn, a unit expected to disband immediately after the mission. Instead it remained as a centre of bombing excellence, tasked with precision attacks and the delivery of new weapons.

The unit dropped a series of Tallboys on the Saumur railway tunnel on June 8, 1944, blocking German reinforcements heading for the D-Day beachhead and between them, Nos 9 and 617 Sqns used the same weapon to capsize *Tirpitz* in a Norwegian fjord. Then, on March 14, 1945, the Dambusters dropped the 22,000lb Grand Slam, or 'earthquake bomb' in anger for the first time, against the Bielefeld viaduct.

Yet it was with Bomber Command's Main Force and the PFF, later No. 8 Group, that the Lancaster made most its significant contribution to Allied victory. The night-bombing campaign – increasingly a day-bombing effort too, as air superiority over Europe was assured – is well known, but the Lancaster also supported the invasion, striking

Finished in the scheme developed for Tiger Force, these 35 Sqn aircraft were involved in a US tour during 1946. Tiger Force had been intended to mount a strategic bombing campaign against Japan, but the atomic strikes in August 1945 brought an end to the war before the Lancasters could engage.

Squadrons Then and Now

Number	Established	Initial Aircraft	Lancaster Service	2017 Role	Aircraft
9 (IX)	December 8, 1914	B.E.2c (from April 1915)	August 1942-July 1946	Offensive Support	Tornado
100	February 23, 1917	F.E.2b	January 1943-May 1946	Offensive Support	Tornado
617	March 21, 1943	Lancaster	March 1943-May 1946	Offensive Support (in process of reformation)	Lighting

The Lancaster's size, multi-engine powerplant and availability made it ideal for a variety of test roles. G-AHJW was engaged in early air-to-air refuelling trials.

The Lancaster Mk II's radial engines gave it a distinctive appearance compared to the Merlin-engined variants. Some 300 Mk IIs were built, of which this was the prototype.

transport nodes and military hubs on the near Continent. After D-Day, Lancasters and the remaining Halifax squadrons even supported the advancing troops, with mass raids on fortified towns and stubborn pockets of resistance. The results overall were devastating – in its wartime career the Lancaster dropped 608,612 tons of bombs.

Lancaster Little Varied

In March 1945, Bomber Command had 56 frontline Lancaster squadrons, with 745 aircraft available for combat and 296 on operational conversion units. In a major production programme, including 430 Mk X aircraft manufactured in Canada, 7,377 Lancasters were built, but in surprisingly few variants. While the Spitfire, for example, spawned a bewildering array of versions, the Lancaster was primarily built as the Merlin-engined Mk I, Bristol Hercules-powered Mk II and Packard Merlin Mk III.

There were variations on these primary themes, including the B.Mk I (Mod) for the Upkeep mine; B.Mk I (FE), specially equipped for operations in the Far East with Tiger Force; B.Mk I (Special) modified to carry the outsize 8,000, 12,000 and 22,000lb bombs; radar-countermeasures Mk VI; and B.Mk VII, with more powerful armament; all were relatively minor by comparison with the major production forms.

It should not be forgotten that the basic Lancaster airframe was also the basis of the York transport, which employed an entirely new fuselage and triple-fin tail, and less radically altered Lancastrian passenger carrier, both of which had important late-war and Berlin Airlift roles. The Lancaster itself also had a major post-war duty, initially operating as the ASR.Mk 3 maritime patrol/search and rescue aircraft with Coastal Command and subsequently as the GR.Mk 3 and MR.Mk 3.

These maritime aircraft filled a sizeable capability gap left when Coastal Command's long-range Consolidated Liberators were returned off Lend Lease, and remained crucial to the front line for a few months after the first Lockheed Neptunes arrived in 1952. Elsewhere, Chadwick had enlarged the Lancaster into the Lincoln for Bomber Command and this in turn evolved into the Shackleton, which replaced the Neptune from 1956. The Shackleton remained on the front line, in the airborne early warning role, until 1991, completing an operational Lancaster legacy of five decades.

Bomber Command had retired the last of its Lancasters, modified as a PR.Mk 1 for photo-mapping duties, in December 1953, while the last operational RAF Lanc of all served the School of Maritime Reconnaissance until October 15, 1956. We are extraordinarily fortunate that BBMF operates PA474, an example of an aircraft that took a decisive role in the fate of a nation. ⊙

Complete with air-droppable Cunliffe-Owen lifeboat, this Lancaster ASR.Mk III was photographed in December 1945.

Lancaster B.Mk I PA474

City of Lincoln

Squadron Leader Clive Rowley MBE RAF (Retd) tells the story of BBMF's Lancaster B.Mk I PA474 City of Lincoln

Lancaster BI PA474 is one of only two airworthy Lancasters remaining from 7,377 built; the other is the Canadian-manufactured B.Mk X FM213 C-GVRA, which flies with the Canadian Warplane Heritage Museum and famously joined BBMF for the 'two-Lancaster summer' of 2014.

PA474 was built at Vickers-Armstrong's Broughton factory on Hawarden airfield, near Chester, and completed on May 31, 1945. The war in Europe had ended a few weeks earlier, so the aircraft was modified for operations with 'Tiger Force' in the Far East and first flown in this configuration in August 1945. But combat in the Far East ended before it could be deployed and instead it was delivered to 38 MU at Llandow for storage, with just three hours ten minutes on the airframe.

Towards the end of June 1947, PA474 was flown to Armstrong Whitworth at Baginton, near Coventry, for conversion to PR1 standard for photographic reconnaissance

Marking both the 70th anniversary of the formation of 617 Sqn 'Dambusters' and its most celebrated raid, PA474 adopted these 617 Sqn colours in 2013. Dual 50 Sqn/460 Sqn markings have replaced them for the 2017 season. Sgt Mobbs/© UK MoD Crown Copyright 2017

Below: In 44 Sqn's care, PA474 was finished in the markings of the aircraft flown by Sqn Ldr Nettleton when he led the low-level Augsburg raid on April 17, 1942. Key Collection

A dorsal mount held experimental aerofoil sections during PA474's time at Cranfield. Key Collection

Ground crew, including Flt Sgt Noel Manning (at left in the cockpit), run W5005's engines up at Binbrook on September 9, 1943. PA474 now wears this 460 Sqn aircraft's markings on its port side. Via BBMF

work. The modifications included removal of the gun turrets, installation of a second pilot's position and radar, and the fitting of cameras in the rear fuselage floor. Metal panels replaced the overhead Perspex panels in the cockpit canopy, to protect against the high temperatures likely to be experienced overseas, and the Lancaster was painted silver.

After modification, PA474 returned to Llandow in early August 1947 and remained there until delivered to Benson for service with 82 Sqn. From September 1948 to February 1952, PA474 served the unit on aerial survey mapping work in East and South Africa, accumulating 2,000 airframe hours before returning to the UK.

Drone Avoidance

The aircraft was loaned to Flight Refuelling at Tarrant Rushden for conversion into a pilotless target drone. It remained with the company for 19 months and underwent a major service prior to the proposed conversion, but the Air Ministry cancelled the modification before any physical work had begun; a Lincoln was used instead and PA474 had been saved from a fate that would almost certainly have seen it destroyed.

Instead it was allocated to the Cranfield College of Aeronautics, a civilian crew flying it there on March 7, 1954. Cranfield modified PA474 as a platform for testing experimental aerofoil sections. It served in this capacity for a decade, but accumulated only 100 hours.

In April 1964, PA474 was grounded and adopted by the Air Historical Branch (AHB) for future display as a static exhibit in the proposed RAF Museum. Following removal of its experimental equipment, the Lancaster was flown to 15 MU at Wroughton for initial restoration and the application of a wartime camouflage scheme. During this period, PA474 also took part in two films, *Operation Crossbow* and *The Guns of Navarone*. Later in 1964, it was flown to Henlow for storage in the open air, awaiting the opening of the new museum.

At this point, the commanding officer of Avro Vulcan-equipped 44 Sqn – which had been the first unit equipped with Lancasters – gained permission from the AHB for PA474 to be transferred into the squadron's care at RAF Waddington. An inspection found the machine structurally sound and authorisation was granted for a single flight from Henlow to Waddington on August 18, 1965.

Over the next ten years the aircraft was refurbished, made fully airworthy and gradually restored to the condition and appearance of a wartime Main Force bomber – by 1975 it had a full set of gun turrets again. PA474 joined the BBMF in 1973, initially at Coltishall, then moved with the Flight to Coningsby in 1976.

The City of Lincoln officially adopted PA474 in 1975 and permission was granted for the aircraft to display the city's name and coat of arms on its nose. Since then, it has always been and will always be so marked, regardless of the wartime colour scheme it wears.

2017 Scheme

After a 'major' maintenance programme during winter 2016/17, PA474 emerged from the Aircraft Restoration Company's hangar at Duxford re-painted with two new identities.

Its port side now represents Lancaster BIII W5005/AR-L *LEADER* of 460 Sqn (Royal Australian Air Force). Its large, colourful nose art depicts a kangaroo wearing wellington boots and playing the bagpipes, representing the mixed nationalities of its crew (Australian, Scottish and Welsh) in July 1943. W5005 flew 51 operations with 460 Sqn and went on to complete a total of 94 'ops' after being transferred to 550 Sqn in May 1944. It was written off after ditching in the Humber Estuary on August 27, 1944, returning from a raid on Kiel.

The BBMF has chosen to represent W5005 as it appeared on September 9, 1943, providing a 'snapshot in time', when its 'bomb log' showed 30 successful operations, including four 'ice cream' tally marks representing raids on Italian targets, and two red bomb symbols for raids on Berlin.

PA474's starboard side now displays the code letters 'VN-T', representing Lancaster LL922, in which Fg Off 'Dougy' Millikin DFC, grandfather of current OC BBMF, Sqn Ldr Andy 'Milli' Millikin, flew 27 of his 35-op tour with 50 Sqn between May and July 1944. 'Dougy' subsequently flew a second operational tour with 156 'Pathfinder' Sqn.

The 'VN-T' codes also honour the sole-surviving member of his crew, wireless operator Warrant Officer John Tait, now 94 years old. LL922 was lost on a bombing raid on August 7/8, 1944, just 12 days after the Millikin crew last flew it. Three of its crew, including pilot Flt Lt Pallandri, were killed. ⊙

Thompson's Vision

Pictured at Martlesham Heath in 1959, Hurricane LF363 was the aeroplane upon which the HAF and ultimately BBMF, were founded. All BBMF Archives/© UK MoD Crown Copyright 2017

Created in a formal ceremony at RAF Biggin Hill on July 11, 1957, the Historic Aircraft Flight laid the foundations for what eventually became the Royal Air Force Battle of Britain Memorial Flight. Former OC BBMF, Sqn Ldr Clive Rowley MBE RAF (Retd), tells the story

Then Station Commander at RAF Biggin Hill, Wing Commander Peter D Thompson DFC was the driving force behind the Historic Aircraft Flight's (HAF's) foundation. He harboured a strongly held belief that the vital importance of the RAF's victory in the Battle of Britain should be commemorated through examples of the principal RAF types involved – the Hurricane and Spitfire – and those who served the RAF, especially the many who sacrificed their lives fighting against tyranny during World War Two, should be remembered. In a letter written to the BBMF in 1999, he modestly recalled: "I did have a hand in collecting together the aircraft that in due time formed the nucleus of what is now the Battle of Britain Memorial Flight."

By the mid-1950s, however, the necessary historic aircraft were in surprisingly short supply. Hurricane LF363, retained somewhat unofficially by the RAF, was now the Service's only airworthy example. Recently overhauled by Hawker and Rolls-Royce free of charge, it was on strength with Biggin Hill's Station Flight, designated as an 'Exhibition Aircraft' on its record card and available as the nucleus of the new HAF. It is probably true to say that without the availability of LF363 in flying condition, the BBMF would never have existed.

Sourcing Spitfires was more problematic. The type had almost completely disappeared from service and the only examples still flying in the UK were three photo-reconnaissance PR.Mk 19s – PM631, PS853 and PS915 – with the civilian-operated Temperature and Humidity (THUM) Flight at Woodvale, Lancashire.

They were scheduled for imminent retirement and grounding, but instead it was decided to allocate them to the HAF, via RAF Duxford. They were due at the Cambridgeshire station on June 12, 1957, but PS915 went unserviceable with an engine problem and PS853 suffered an engine failure on take-off and ended up "taking a header into the ground", to quote a contemporary newspaper report. The mishaps were perhaps

Thompson, Rankin and Johnson at Biggin Hill on July 11, having safely delivered the Spitfires from Duxford.

After a couple of mishaps, the Spitfires flew into Biggin Hill on July 11, 1957. Hunter F5s from 41 Sqn (left) and Javelins from 46 Sqn provided escort.

indicative of the aircrafts' poor condition, but with rectification and repairs complete, the Spitfires were made ready for the move to Biggin.

Three-ship Formation

The machines were flown from Duxford to Biggin Hill as a three-ship formation on July 11, the day of the HAF's founding. The RAF's highest scoring ace, Group Captain JE 'Johnnie' Johnson DSO and two Bars, DFC and Bar (later Air Vice-Marshal CB CBE DSO and two bars DFC and Bar) led the formation in PS853.

Another famous, high-scoring RAF ace, Group Captain (later Air Commodore) James Rankin DSO and Bar, DFC and Bar, flew PM631 in one of his last duties before he retired from the RAF in 1958. As the most junior of the trio, Peter Thompson was left to fly PS915, which the others felt was not in the best shape! This was subsequently confirmed and it was retired from flying almost immediately. It remained grounded until 1986, then joined the BBMF in April 1987.

Three No. 41 Sqn Hunter F5s from Biggin Hill and three No. 46 Sqn Gloster Javelins from RAF Odiham met the Spitfire formation en route and escorted it to Biggin Hill. The Mk 19s landed at 11:00hrs; Air Officer Commanding-in-Chief (AOC-in-C) of Fighter Command, Air Marshal Sir Thomas Pike KCB CBE DFC and Bar was there to greet them.

With Spitfire PS853 as backdrop, the AOC-in-C announced the formation of the Historic Aircraft Flight, although it was already being referred to, not least in the RAF Biggin Hill *Operations Record* (F540) for that day, as the 'Battle of Britain Flight', a title that became official the following February.

Voluntary Basis

Although Peter Thompson had gained the necessary high-level approval to form the HAF, it was made clear that there would be no public funding and no established manpower for the maintenance and operation of its aircraft. It was to be operated on an entirely voluntary basis. Thompson asked his OC Engineering Wing at Biggin Hill, Squadron »

The THUM Flight Mk 19s at Woodvale in June 1957. Their continued airworthiness was somewhat questionable!

Group Captain Peter D Thompson DFC

Thompson had joined the RAF Volunteer Reserve in January 1939, aged 18. He flew Hawker Hurricanes with No. 605 Sqn, Auxiliary Air Force (AuxAF), during the final weeks of the Battle of Britain and then in Malta with Nos 261 and 185 Sqns between April 1941 and January 1942. After his Hurricane was badly damaged in combat he was forced to bale out at very low level over the island, so low in fact that both he and his aircraft landed in the same field; he described it as "A close run thing".

On his return to the UK, Thompson was awarded the Distinguished Flying Cross (DFC). He was 'rested' for a period as an instructor and then as a test pilot in the Middle East. From 1943 he served as a Flight Commander with 601 Sqn, AuxAF, flying Spitfires in North Africa, Sicily and Italy.

Again back in the UK, he took command of 129 Sqn in July 1944, a command he held until April 1945. Operating from RAF Ford, flying North American Mustang Mk IIIs, he destroyed three V-1 flying bombs and damaged two more. His final wartime 'tally' was three enemy aircraft destroyed (plus three V-1s), two shared destroyed, two probably destroyed and four (plus two V-1s) damaged.

Peter Thompson remained in the RAF on a permanent commission after the war and flew Gloster Meteor and Hawker Hunter jet fighters. Peacetime military flying was not without its risks though, and he had to abandon an aircraft for the second time in his career when a US Air Force F-86 Sabre knocked the tail of his Meteor in a mid-air collision – he landed by parachute in a Guildford street.

In 1955 he was posted to RAF Biggin Hill as the Wing Commander Flying and in 1956 became Station Commander when it became a Wing Commander Station. In 1958 he was posted away from Biggin Hill and what had by then become the Battle of Britain Flight.

Thompson's final RAF appointment was as Air Attaché at the British Embassy in Lima, Peru. He retired as a group captain in September 1975 and settled in Menorca. He died on March 2, 2003, aged 82, leaving a lasting legacy of national importance – the Battle of Britain Memorial Flight.

Thompson managed to secure the HAF's first 'fighter' Spitfires in the form of three Mk 16s. Here he poses in one of their cockpits at Biggin Hill in 1957.

Thompson flew the jet-powered Meteor after World War Two.

Thompson, fourth from left, with 601 Sqn aircrew and a Spitfire Mk IX in Italy during 1944.

Squadrons Then and Now

Number	Established	Initial aircraft	Aircraft in 1940	Aircraft in 1957	2017 Role	Aircraft
41	July 14, 1916	F.B.5	Spitfire I & II	Hunter F5	Test & Evaluation	Tornado and Typhoon
605	October 15, 1926	DH.9A	Hurricane I & II	Vampire FB5	Logistics and policing	None

Leader EH Sowden (later Wing Commander Sowden MBE), who had worked as an RAF engineer on Hurricanes and Spitfires during the war, for help. In addition to his 'day job' organising the maintenance of the station's Hunters, Sowden assembled and led a team of suitably experienced volunteer tradesmen to work on the HAF's aircraft and set about sourcing spares.

But Thompson and others were not entirely happy that the only Spitfires available were unarmed photo-reconnaissance machines not at all representative of the type's fighter variants. He therefore persuaded the authorities to allocate three ground-demonstration Mk 16s from storage. Thompson believed the aeroplanes could be made airworthy relatively easily; Sowden agreed. The engineer also knew that spares were more readily available for the Mk 16s and gave them priority. First to fly in HAF hands was TE330, which Thompson air tested in September 1957.

Air Officer Commanding-in-Chief Fighter Command, Air Marshal Sir Thomas Pike KCB CBE DFC and Bar, formally creates the HAF at Biggin Hill on July 11, 1957.

Thompson's Legacy

By 1958, when Thompson was posted away from Biggin Hill, the Battle of Britain Flight comprised Hurricane LF363; Spitfire Mk 16s TE330, TE476 and SL674; and Spitfire PR.Mk 19 PM631. He left the Flight on a firm footing, having laid the foundations for its subsequent growth into the established unit that is so well-known and loved today. The RAF and the millions of people who see BBMF aircraft flying today owe a debt of gratitude to Peter Thompson, for his foresight and determination in 1957.

In 1998 he visited the BBMF at RAF Coningsby and was delighted to find the Flight still operating, more than 41 years after he set it up, but as an established unit with its own hangar... "No longer tucked away in a cluttered corner of the Station Flight hangar, but a proud display in immaculate surroundings." ʘ

Without Squadron Leader Sowden's engineering skills there would have been no HAF or BBMF. He is at the centre of this 1959 Battle of Britain Flight groundcrew group.

TE330 was among the three Spitfire Mk 16s that Sowden returned to airworthiness.

Keeping Them Flying BBMF Engineering

A typical October day at Coningsby, in this case during 2015, has Spitfires P7350 and AB910 receiving attention. Clive Rowley

The Battle of Britain Memorial Flight maintains 12 irreplaceable historic aircraft in airworthy condition. Their ongoing preservation is planned on a long-term basis, with the ultimate aim of keeping them flying forever. These are perhaps the most cared-for aircraft in the world; they are certainly maintained to a much higher standard than was possible during World War Two. Former Officer Commanding BBMF, Sqn Ldr Clive Rowley MBE RAF (Retd), explains how it's done

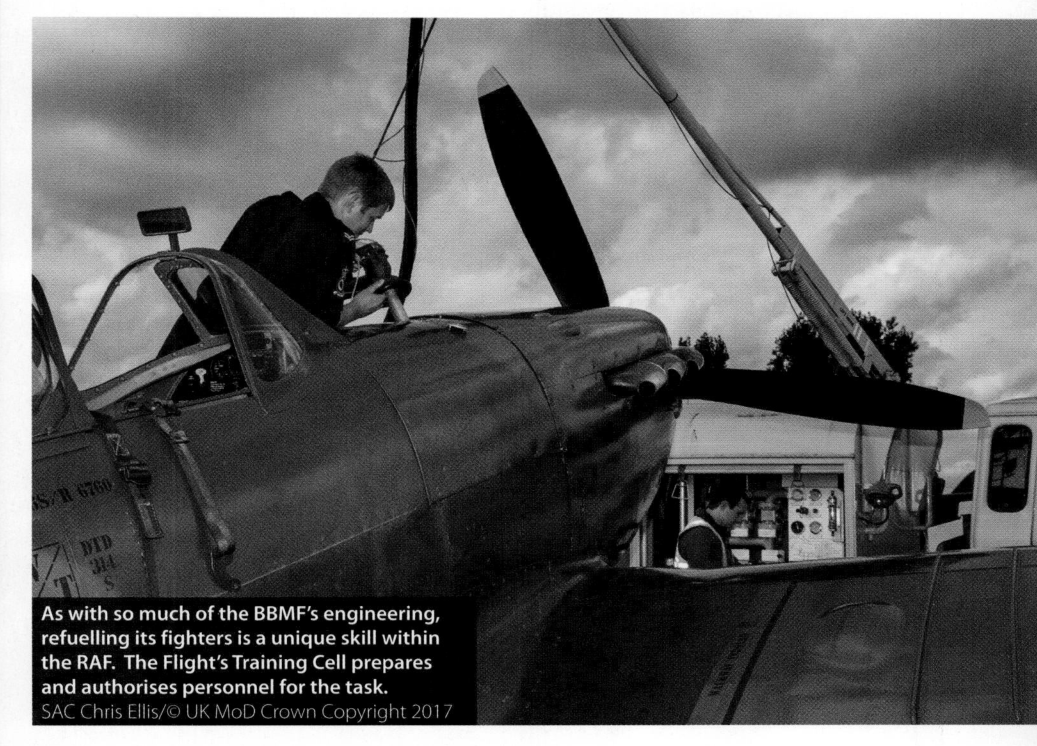

As with so much of the BBMF's engineering, refuelling its fighters is a unique skill within the RAF. The Flight's Training Cell prepares and authorises personnel for the task.
SAC Chris Ellis/© UK MoD Crown Copyright 2017

The BBMF Engineering Team comprises just 30 RAF technicians, headed by the Flight's Engineering Officer (a warrant officer). He and his engineering management team of a flight sergeant, two Full Time Reserve Service (FTRS) chief technicians and three Regular RAF sergeants, are responsible for the Flight's engineering standards and safety, and for co-ordinating aircraft servicing and maintenance programmes.

The Flight's other RAF technicians form the 'Mechanical Team' and the 'Avionics Team'. The Mechanical Team is the larger of the two and specialises in aircraft structures (airframes, flying controls, hydraulic and pneumatic systems) and propulsion systems (engines and propellers, fuel, oil, ignition and cooling systems). The Avionics Team is responsible for maintaining and, when necessary, upgrading the electrical and avionics systems on the Flight's aircraft, ranging from simple magnetic compasses to modern retrofitted equipment, including Mode S IFF transponders, radios, GPS and traffic-alerting systems.

The attractions of this unique, challenging, yet rewarding engineering environment mean there is a long waiting list of Regular RAF technicians looking to be posted to the Flight. Everyone who joins the relatively small engineering team is a volunteer and the normal tour of duty is three to five years.

A small cadre of embedded FTRS technicians provides a core of experience in maintaining these historic aircraft. They have many decades of BBMF experience, each having served with the Flight for 20 to 30 years.

The BBMF's engineers are dedicated professionals who passionately support the belief that, although the debt of gratitude can never be repaid, as long as the Flight's aircraft are kept flying they will be a lasting memorial to those who have gone before.

The BBMF Year

BBMF splits the year into roughly equal halves. During the flying/display season from April to the end of September, the emphasis is on ensuring the required number and type of aircraft are available to meet display commitments. The Flight routinely deploys aircraft and engineering support teams away for several days at a time, especially when displaying at more distant venues, minimising the expenditure of strictly controlled flying hours in transiting back and forth.

During the winter servicing period – from October to March – the majority of the Flight's aircraft (except the Chipmunks) are grounded for the extensive maintenance that prepares them for the next display season and ensures their long-term preservation. Usually, at least one aircraft is scheduled to undergo a 'major' maintenance programme each year, under contract and away from Coningsby.

Training The New For The Old

Engineering the BBMF's historic aircraft is quite different to engineering modern frontline RAF equipment. The Defence School of Technical Training at RAF Cosford long since ceased teaching the 'old fashioned' skill sets required to keep BBMF flying. For example, RAF mechanical technicians are now trained only on jet or turboprop engines – all the BBMF's aircraft have piston engines. Working on the front line, RAF tradesmen become used to modern aircraft that self diagnose faults. If a component is unserviceable it is usually easily replaced and they will seldom be involved in fault diagnosis or the 'deep' servicing of components, which is normally carried out by contractors.

The BBMF therefore trains its engineers on the job, through a Training and Standards Cell run by three of the Flight's NCO technicians. Their remit is to give engineers new to the »

Of the Flight's aircraft, only the Dakota has radial engines. Newly posted engineers learn the exacting requirements of BBMF maintenance under the watchful eye of experienced NCOs. Sgt Andy Benson/© UK MoD Crown Copyright 2017

Flight the best possible training, enabling them to work safely and effectively on the BBMF's beautiful old aeroplanes. They deliver academic instruction in relevant theory and hands-on technical training, leading to specific engineering authorisations.

The formal academic instruction includes the basic theory of piston engines and of the BBMF engine types, and the health and safety implications of maintaining BBMF aircraft, focussing strongly on the safety issues associated with propellers and magneto ignition systems. The lack of redundancy and paucity of back-up systems for safety-critical components on aircraft of this vintage is also stressed. While modern aircraft have multiple back-up systems should things start to fail, there are very little if any duplicate systems in components such as the flying controls on the BBMF aircraft.

The Flight is governed by exactly the same regulations as the rest of the RAF in terms of training and qualifications to undertake engineering tasks. The Training Cell corporals provide this training and award specific engineering authorisations for tasks including aircraft refuelling or the preparation of an aircraft for flight. The Training Cell also runs trade qualification – 'Q' – courses for Flight technicians, which, on successful completion of examinations, entitle the tradesman to an RAF-wide 'competency' certification on the BBMF's aircraft, valid for five years. Subsequently, suitably qualified individuals can be identified as candidates to fill future posts on the Flight. This system helps ensure BBMF will always have sufficient personnel with the correct skill sets to call upon, especially in supervisory and training posts.

Even the BBMF's ground handling is unusual in the modern Royal Air Force – groundcrew rarely tow aircraft backwards elsewhere! SAC Jack Welson/© UK MoD Crown Copyright 2017

Spares

"What about spare parts?" It's a question visitors to the BBMF's hangar often ask as they wonder how the Flight replaces faulty or worn-out parts on its old aircraft. The BBMF has a healthy stock of spare parts at its RAF Coningsby base. They are stored in airworthy condition, catalogued and recorded on the RAF supply database, and controlled by a team of supply personnel, both in the station Supply Squadron and on the Flight. Inevitably though, some spares are not available from stock. The long-term management and procurement of spares is the responsibility of the BBMF Project Team. This small group of civil servants, contractors and an RAF chief technician is based at Coningsby and responsible for maintaining the operating safety case for each aeroplane, project managing the major maintenance contracts and implementing aircraft modifications.

In order to avoid the possibility of the Flight running out of critical spares, regular meetings are held to identify the items that, if not available, could potentially lead to aircraft being grounded. It would be a false economy and not very practical to have a spare of absolutely everything for every type, so the engineers work with the Project Team and Coningsby's supply personnel to identify and prioritise the spares that are going to be required and that may be difficult to obtain, possibly with long lead times. This creates the need to identify manufacturers willing to produce items, possibly in very small quantities, with a minimal profit margin.

The BBMF engineering effort is supported by a number of small- to medium-sized companies, generally operating with a small but highly skilled, dedicated workforce. They all hold the necessary accreditations that ensure they produce or overhaul spares to the required standard. Most also supply the civilian warbird community and as such are required to hold the necessary Civil Aviation Authority accreditations.

The combination of a good stock of spare parts and the ability to have parts made when required, ensures the aim of keeping the BBMF's aircraft flying forever will not be prevented by a shortage of replacement components.

In some cases, the very latest technology combines with the old airframes to deliver an optimal engineering solution. Sensors gather parametric data on multiple systems for download and subsequent analysis on a laptop. Cpl Paul Robertshaw/© UK MoD Crown Copyright 2017

Above: Parts are carefully managed. This is a Dakota crankshaft. Sgt Mobbs/© UK MoD Crown Copyright 2017

Engines

Although it means they are no longer strictly authentic, most BBMF aircraft are not fitted with their original engine mark. Driven by availability, ease of maintenance and management, and to enable the rationalisation of logistic support, the aircraft have been grouped and modified where required to enable the use of common engine marks as far as possible. The result is that the Spitfire Mk II and V are powered by the Rolls-Royce Merlin 35 (instead of the original Mk XII and Mk 45, respectively); the Mk IX and XVI Spitfires both run the Packard Merlin 266 (which strictly speaking and confusingly makes the Mk IX a Mk XVI); the Mk XIX Spitfires are fitted with the Rolls-Royce Griffon Mk 58 RG30 SM-S (a modified Avro Shackleton engine), and the Hurricanes and Lancaster have Merlin 25, 225 or 500 engines, which have a common build standard, configuration and power output. »

The Rolls-Royce Merlin is ubiquitous among the BBMF fleet, powering the Hurricanes, Lancaster and all but two of the Spitfires. This engine has the three-pot exhausts of the Merlin 35. SAC Jack Nelson/© UK MoD Crown Copyright 2017

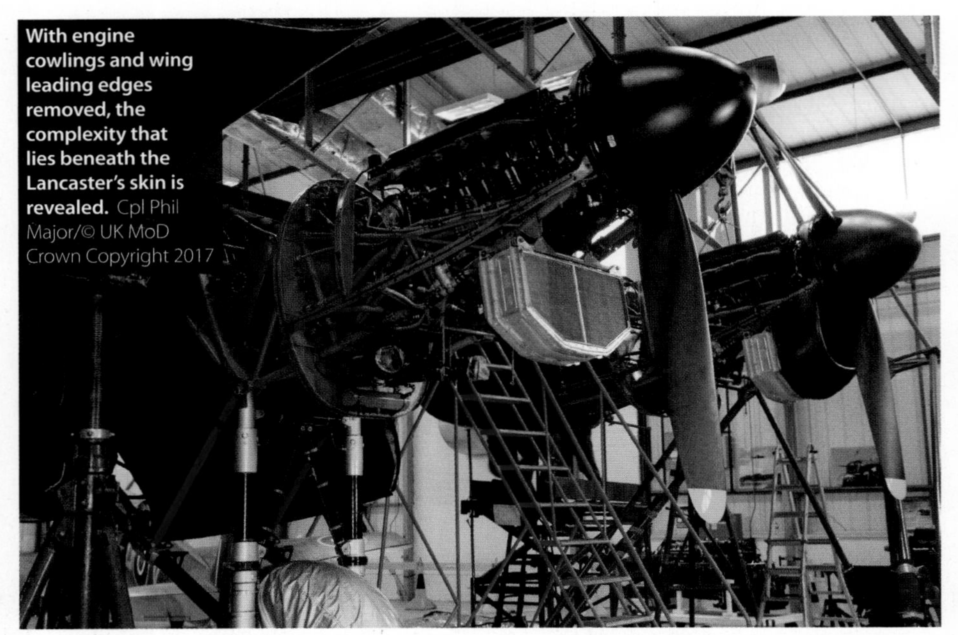

With engine cowlings and wing leading edges removed, the complexity that lies beneath the Lancaster's skin is revealed. Cpl Phil Major/© UK MoD Crown Copyright 2017

With a total BBMF pool of 17 Merlin and Griffon engines, spare engines of the appropriate mark are usually readily available, on-hand should an unscheduled engine change be required. This occurs infrequently given the Flight's generally good reliability and it is not unusual for engines to reach their installed life limit, which is now set at 500 flying hours (considerably less than the original limits). This is not a finite life, however, and at this point an in-depth reconditioning can be carried out, enabling re-lifing for a further 500 hours.

The Project Team, responsible for managing all major maintenance contracts, currently uses Gloucestershire-based Retro Track and Air (UK) for its engine repair and overhaul work. In addition to completing full engine overhauls, the company has the capability to manufacture components, including camshafts, pistons and running gear. In essence, if a technical drawing exists, an item can be produced to the original manufacturer's specification, while pattern parts can also be made using reverse engineering techniques. On completion of an engine overhaul, the company carries out comprehensive testing using a custom-built dynamometer test bed, a procedure that identifies leaks or emergent faults and gives significant confidence in the product.

Clearly, engines are a critical item with regard to airworthiness, with no redundancy in terms of safety in the single-engined aircraft, so it is essential they are maintained to the highest possible standards.

Modern regulations

In common with all current British military aircraft, the regulatory framework imposed by the Military Aviation Authority (MAA) governs the BBMF's machines. Thus, each undergoes an annual Military Airworthiness Review (MAR), similar to the MOT required for a car. An independent check carried out by a contracted company, it consists of a comprehensive review of all the relevant documented aircraft records and a physical survey of the machine, leading to the award of a MAR certificate. Without a valid MAR certificate the aeroplanes are not permitted to fly.

This process is identical to that applied to the most modern aircraft and is indicative of how BBMF engineering has to be conducted to exactly the same standards and in accordance with the regulations applied to all RAF aircraft, regardless of the fact that the Flight's warbirds are all more than 70 years old. This compliance with modern regulations will ensure the aeroplanes remain airworthy and fit for purpose well into the future and provides the necessary confidence in that continuing airworthiness. ⊙

January 2017, and BBMF's engineer's enter the New Year working hard to prepare the aircraft for their first flights of the year, just two or three months away. Clive Rowley

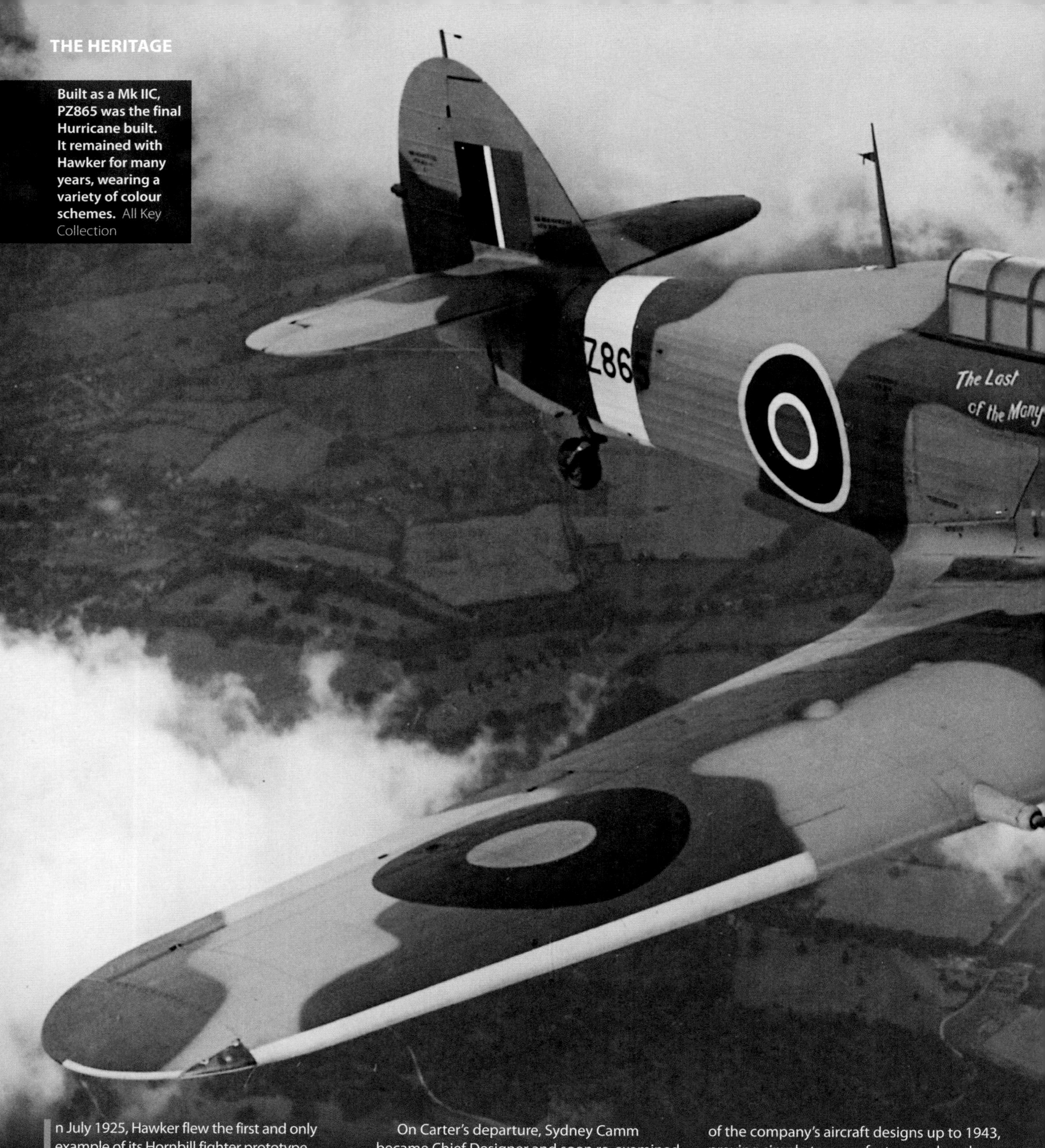

Built as a Mk IIC, PZ865 was the final Hurricane built. It remained with Hawker for many years, wearing a variety of colour schemes. All Key Collection

In July 1925, Hawker flew the first and only example of its Hornbill fighter prototype. Unusually for a period when the RAF preferred its fighters to have radial engines, the diminutive machine featured a close-cowled inline, but was otherwise externally unremarkable.

Under its sheet metal and canvas skin, the Hornbill was of mixed wood and metal construction, its welded steel tube forward fuselage structure representing Hawker's first use of such technology. Possessed of useful low-speed handling characteristics, the Hornbill nonetheless failed as a fighting aeroplane, while its designer, Wilfred Carter, left Hawker not long after its maiden flight.

On Carter's departure, Sydney Camm became Chief Designer and soon re-examined the Hornbill's metal structure. With the RAF's airframe maintenance organisation heavily geared towards woodworking, Camm judged welded steel tube too difficult for regular service use. However, tubular metal could be used to create extremely strong assemblies, with the promise of weight savings compared to wooden equivalents.

Camm therefore worked with engineer Fred Sigrist to develop a system of tubes and joining plates that could be adapted to suit any of Hawker's designs. Known as the 'Hawker metal construction', it was used on every one of the company's aircraft designs up to 1943, proving simple to manufacture and, perhaps more importantly, repair at squadron level.

The technique was employed on minor prototypes before appearing in three stunning prototypes at the 1929 Olympia Aero Show – the Hawker Hart bomber, Hornet fighter and Tomtit trainer all promised to set new standards in their fields. In the event, the Tomtit was built in limited numbers and ultimately lost out to Avro's Tutor, but the Hart sired a series of world-class multi-role aircraft that served into the early years of World War Two, and the Hornet evolved into the superlative Fury.

Hurrah Hurricane

Through the successful application of tried and trusted construction to a modern airframe configuration, powerful engine and multi-gun armament, Hawker's Sydney Camm created the Hurricane, first of the RAF's modern fighters

Monoplane Machinations

By now, the Air Ministry was beginning to realise that the latest bomber designs flew at speeds and altitudes where they were extremely difficult for in-service fighters to catch. Its solution to the problem was summarised in specification F.7/30 of 1930, which called for a fighter capable of 250mph and a doubling of standard armament to four 0.303in machine guns.

These were radical requirements when Bristol's Bulldog, the latest RAF fighter, was carrying its two guns to only a little over 170mph, yet senior Air Ministry officials and RAF policy makers remained deeply suspicious of the monoplane layout even though it clearly offered potentially dramatic performance improvements.

Manufacturers, including Hawker and Supermarine, submitted F.7/30 designs, but the specification foundered for being based on the complex and unreliable Rolls-Royce Goshawk engine. Instead, the Fury was built in considerable numbers by the standards of the time and the radial-engined, twin-gun Gloster Gauntlet finally evolved from F.7/30 thinking.

Meanwhile, industry, including Sydney Camm, was convinced of the performance advantages inherent in the monoplane layout. In 1933, Camm therefore began studies into such a fighter, based on the Fury. The so-called Fury Monoplane retained the proven tubular structure and majority fabric covering, and featured four machine guns and an enclosed cockpit, but retained the disastrous Goshawk powerplant.

As late 1933 turned into early 1934, Camm managed to illicit tentative Air Ministry interest in his monoplane scheme, just as Rolls-Royce provided preliminary data on its PV.12, an engine that matured as the legendary Merlin. It was an obvious match for the Hawker fighter, which now became the Interceptor Monoplane. Official guidance still reco[illegible]ended four-gun weaponry, but Camm

Flying from RAF Coltishall, 257 Sqn used its Hurricane Mk Is to patrol over Britain's North Sea fishing fleets and on offensive operations into Europe. The Norfolk station saw a good deal of snow in January 1941.

K5083 was the Hurricane prototype. Here it has the original two-bladed propeller and retractable tailwheel, but the tailplane bracing struts have been removed. A radio antenna has been added, although the aircraft still lacks the distinctive ventral fin.

was convinced of the need for more guns; it is well worth noting that while Hawker was working hard to interest the Air Ministry and RAF that a step change in fighter design was inevitable, the Ministry's German equivalent was issuing official requirements for exactly the type of aircraft Camm was proposing.

By late summer 1934, Hawker had a mock-up ready for inspection and against this the Air Ministry drew up specification F.36/34 for a Single Seat Fighter. A prototype was ordered on February 21, 1935 and although thoughts were now turning to the possibility of eight-gun armament, no weapons were to be fitted.

The machine flew for the first time on November 6, powered by a Merlin 'C' engine. By the following June, the new fighter had been named Hurricane and the Air Ministry ordered an initial batch of 600 to Mk I standard. With considerable foresight, Hawker had actually begun tooling up to produce 1,000 Hurricanes and although a change to the Merlin III for production aircraft caused early delays, once it began, production was rapid. By the end of 1937, the Hurricane had begun replacing 111 Sqn's Gauntlets.

Hurricane in a Hurry

Although the Spitfire proved the higher-performing, more adaptable and undoubtedly prettier aeroplane, there should be no doubting the advance in fighter capability encapsulated by the Hurricane. Camm's decision to use structural techniques pioneered as early as 1925 enabled rapid development contrary to official opinion. His foresight in choosing the PV.12 engine and making provision for eight machine guns delivered a fighter more than 60mph faster than the RAF's best in-service machine (the Gloster Gladiator) and with twice the punch.

History records that the Hurricane, flying with the majority of Fighter Command's squadrons, played the major defensive role over Southeast England and the Channel during the Battle of Britain. For that reason alone it might be considered the most significant fighter in British, if not world history, yet the harsh combat of summer 1940 was but the beginning of the Hurricane's fighting career.

Hurricane Force

The Hurricane Mk I had undergone considerable improvement even before the Battle of Britain, with the more powerful Merlin III, along with a three-bladed, variable-pitch propeller that replaced the original two-bladed, fixed-pitch unit. Metal-skinned wings were introduced on the production lines from 1939, replacing the fabric-covered aerofoils with which the type entered service.

Now the aircraft's evolution began closely following Rolls-Royce's engine developments, and the two-stage supercharged Merlin XX first flew in a Hurricane in June 1940. Delivered from September 4, the Hurricane Mk IIA used the improved engine's greater power to achieve higher performance, while the Mk IIB carried four extra machine guns.

With the Mk II came an indication of the Hurricane's nascent ground-attack capability. The aircraft's performance in the air-to-air arena had proven sufficiently adequate during the Battle, but the latest German fighter developments were outpacing its dated design – the Spitfire was clearly superior in fighter versus fighter combat.

But with more powerful fixed armament and underwing pylons for bombs, the Hurricane

There were several two-seat Hurricanes, including the Persian Two-Seat Trainer. Hawker built two, delivering them in 1947 for the advanced fighter training role.

Only three prototypes of the Hurricane Mk V were built. Their weapons included the 40mm gun option shown here and power came from a 1,700hp Merlin 32, but problems with overheating, plus the ready availability of Mk II and IV airframes, saw the variant cancelled.

Equipped with drop tanks for extended range, the Hurricane Mk IIC was formidable in the night-intruder role, ranging over the continent from its British bases.

Right: Canadian Car and Foundry built Hurricanes for the RAF and Royal Canadian Air Force. Propeller spinners were often left off in Canada, as these 1 Operational Training Unit Hurricane Mk XIIs illustrate.

became a formidable ground-attack machine, ready to take an important role in the offensive operations that saw RAF fighters roaming over the near continent from the end of 1940. The Mk IIC replaced the machine guns with four 20mm cannon and their devastating use against ground targets paved the way for the radical Hurricane Mk IID.

Equipped with a pair of 40mm Vickers 'S' guns, the Hurricane IID famously became a tank-buster par excellence over the deserts of North Africa. The heavy weapons and their draggy installation slowed the aircraft to the point where it required fighter escort, but with brave, determined pilots, the Mk IID was the scourge of Axis armour.

In 1943, the Hurricane Mk IV entered production alongside the IIC. Powered by a 1,620hp Merlin 24 or 27 (compared to the 1,030hp Merlin III of the Mk I), the Mk IV featured a universal wing equipped with two machine guns as standard, plus fittings for the 40mm Vickers, bombs or rocket projectiles according to operational requirements. The Mk IV was also heavily armour plated for survivability in its primary attack mission.

With the North African war at an end, it famously served on with No. 6 Sqn, its greatest exponent in the anti-armour role, as the Allies fought their way through Italy. The Mk II and IV Hurricanes were also key components in the fight against Japanese aggression in the Far East. Flying in the European Theatre, both marks employed rockets with considerable success into 1944 before another Hawker product, the infamous Typhoon, took over the role.

The Hurricane was also built extensively in Canada, while the Sea Hurricane was manufactured at home. Compared to the Seafire, the naval Spitfire variant, the Sea Hurricane was always the superior aircraft around the deck, thanks to the stability assured by its wide-track landing gear.

That same trait made for easier, safer ground handling on the grass airfields of the period, especially at night, and the Hurricane was easily superior to the Spitfire for nocturnal operations. With the Mk II these spilled over into night intruding over occupied Europe and in many ways the Hurricane squadrons pioneered the tactics that the RAF came to rely on before and after the D-Day operation.

Today the Hurricane is well represented in museum collections and although airworthy examples are rare compared to the Spitfire, for example, several are maintained in flyable condition. The Hurricane's relatively benign ground handling is as valuable today as it was during World War Two, with pilots new to the BBMF's fighters initially converting onto its Mk IIs to gain experience in a powerful tail-dragger aircraft.

Number 6 Squadron retired the last of the RAF's frontline Hurricanes in 1947, replacing them with the Hawker Tempest F6. The unit's tank-busting with the Mk IID earned it the 'Flying Tin-openers' nickname and a squadron badge was designed to suit; it's a marking proudly displayed on 6 Sqn's Lossiemouth-based Eurofighter Typhoons today. ⊙

The Sea Hurricane was a vital fleet defence tool until more advanced Seafires and US-sourced types began replacing it. This Sea Hurricane was aboard HMS *Argus*, a training vessel, in 1943.

Squadrons Then and Now

Number	Established	Initial Aircraft	Hurricane Service	2017 Role	Aircraft
6	January 31, 1914	Martinsyde S.1	February 1941-January 1947	Air Defence & Offensive Support	Typhoon

Prior to its BBMF service, ZA947 flew with the Royal Aircraft Establishment. Key Collection

Today, the Dakota's interior is closer to its World War Two configuration than it was during its time with the RAE. Cpl Phil Major/© UK MoD Crown Copyright 2017

Dakota C.Mk 3 ZA947

Squadron Leader Clive Rowley MBE RAF (Retd) tells the story of BBMF's Dakota C.Mk 3 ZA947

Dakota C.Mk 3 ZA947 is the last of its type serving the Royal Air Force, which once operated more than 1,900 'Daks'. Douglas built the machine as a C-47A Skytrain at its Long Beach, California facility in 1942. It was delivered to the US Army Air Force with the serial number 42-24338 on September 7, 1943. A little over a week later, on September 16 it was transferred to the Royal Canadian Air Force (RCAF) and re-designated as a Dakota Mk III, with serial number 661.

Dakota 661 served out World War Two entirely in Canada. Little is known of its duties, although it is thought to have flown with 164 Sqn, one of the RCAF's premier transport units, based at Moncton, New Brunswick. From Moncton, 164 Sqn's work involved moving passengers and freight around Newfoundland, particularly to Goose Bay and Gander. The Dakotas and their crews operated

ZA947 is marked as 233 Sqn's FZ692 *KWICHERBICHEN*, complete with 'invasion stripes' for the D-Day operation in June 1944. Cpl Phil Major/© UK MoD Crown Copyright 2017

Earlier in its BBMF career, ZA947 was painted to represent the 271 Sqn aircraft in which Flt Lt David Lord and crew made two supply drops during the battle of Arnhem, despite mortal hits to their aircraft, which crashed soon after. Lord was posthumously awarded the Victoria Cross for his actions. Key Collection

in extreme weather conditions, flying over inhospitable terrain to complete their tasks.

Post-war, Dakota 661 supported Canadian forces in Europe between 1965 and 1969, when it was declared surplus to Canadian Armed Forces requirements and sold to Scottish Aviation at Prestwick, for operation on behalf of the Royal Aircraft Establishment (RAE). Since its Canadian identity did not comply with standard RAF serials, the Dakota was given the RAF serial KG661.

For some years KG661 was based with the RAE at West Freugh, a coastal airfield in Wigtownshire, near Portpatrick, 5 miles southeast of Stranraer in Dumfries and Galloway, Scotland. From West Freugh it was used in various trials over the Luce Bay ranges, and particularly for dropping experimental sonobuoys into the sea and launching remotely-piloted vehicles. The aircraft was given the name *Portpatrick Princess*.

Identity Crisis

In the late 1970s it was realised that KG661 had, in fact, belonged to another Dakota, which had crashed and been written off. In July 1979, therefore, 'KG661' was reserialled ZA947, which explains why the BBMF Dakota wears a serial that falls immediately after those of a batch of Puma helicopters and before a Westland Lynx!

In its later years of RAE service, ZA947 was based at Farnborough and fitted with a stronger floor and 'modern' airliner-style seats from a de Havilland Comet. But the aircraft was damaged at Farnborough in 1990, when the navigator accidentally retracted the landing gear on the ground while the engines were running. As the undercarriage collapsed, the port propeller hit the ground, destroying the reduction gearbox; debris smashed into the fuselage and the aircraft's port wing was damaged beyond repair.

A contract to repair and overhaul the aircraft was awarded to Air Atlantique. A port wing was obtained from a derelict Dakota in Malta and brought to UK. It was badly corroded and the company re-skinned much of it and replaced several ribs and other components of its internal structure. The refurbished wing was then taken to Farnborough and fitted to ZA947, together with a new engine and propeller. Once it was flyable, the aircraft was ferried to Coventry for a complete overhaul.

The Defence Research Agency, successor to the RAE, subsequently declared ZA947 surplus to requirements and offered it for disposal in 1992. RAF Strike Command took the aircraft on, for issue to the BBMF. It was taken on the Flight's charge in March 1993.

Perhaps originally intended as a BBMF support and training aircraft, the Dakota replaced the Flight's de Havilland Devon C1, which was auctioned off in 1998. With no other multi-engine tailwheel aircraft in RAF service outside the BBMF, the Dakota soon became an important training asset for new Lancaster crew and for renewing the Bomber pilots' currency each year. But it has also become a sought-after display aircraft, appearing regularly on the airshow circuit and at commemorative events. ⊙

AB910's markings commemorate Spitfire VB BM327/SH-F *peterjohn. 'I'*, the personal aircraft of 64 Sqn's Flt Lt Tony Cooper in 1944.
Jim Dooley Photography

Spitfire Mk VB AB910

Squadron Leader Clive Rowley MBE RAF (Retd) tells the story of BBMF's Spitfire Mk VB AB910

Spitfire AB910 was among the initial batch of 500 Mk VB aircraft ordered from Supermarine's Castle Bromwich factory. Fitted with two 20mm cannon, four 0.303in Browning machine guns and a Rolls-Royce Merlin 45 engine, it was delivered to its first operational unit, No. 222 (Natal) Squadron, at North Weald, on August 22, 1941.

Within days of its arrival the aircraft was damaged in a forced landing at Lympne. After repair it was re-allocated to 130 Sqn at Perranporth, Cornwall, for convoy protection patrols and fighter escort to daylight bombing raids.

In June 1942, AB910 was delivered to 133 (Eagle) Sqn at Biggin Hill. It flew 29 operational sorties with the unit, including four on August 19, 1942 during the fierce aerial battles in support of the Dieppe Raid. One of AB910's pilots that day, American Flight Sergeant 'Dixie' Alexander was credited with destroying a Dornier Do 217 bomber in the aircraft.

Up with LF363 in June 2004, AB910 wears the desert camouflage and personal 'IR-G' codes of Wing Commander Ian Gleed's Mk VB. Sgt Jack Pritchard/© UK MoD Crown Copyright 2017

In the mid-1970s, AB910 was marked as 'QJ-J' for 92 Sqn. Note the inaccurate exhaust and propeller installations. Key Collection

AB910 flew operationally into July 1944, serving with 242 Sqn, and then with 416 and 402 (RCAF) Squadrons. With the latter the aircraft flew numerous cover patrols over the Normandy invasion beachheads on D-Day, June 6, 1944, and subsequently. In almost three years of frontline duties, AB910 flew a remarkable 143 operational missions and it was damaged on four separate occasions in landing or taxiing incidents.

Margaret Hangs On

On July 13, 1944, AB910's long operational flying career came to an end and it was transferred to 53 OTU at Hibaldstow, where it served to the end of the war. On February 14, 1945, the aircraft famously flew with a person on its tail…

Leading Aircraftswoman Margaret Horton, a Women's Auxiliary Air Force aircraft mechanic, had sat on the aircraft's tail as it taxied out to the take-off point (a standard practice in windy weather). The pilot, Flight Lieutenant Neill Cox DFC and Bar, did not know she was there and took off with Margaret hanging on. The combination of her weight on the tail and grip on the elevator very nearly had disastrous results, but Cox maintained control and one circuit later, landed with Margaret wrapped around the fin!

After the war, AB910 served for a year as a radar calibration 'target' aircraft with 527 Sqn and then with the Radio Warfare Establishment. In 1947, Group Captain Allen Wheeler bought it and the aircraft was flown privately as an air racer for six years, registered G-AISU and fitted with a four-bladed propeller. During this period, AB910 was damaged twice more in ground incidents.

Vickers-Armstrong purchased it in 1953. After a full refurbishment, renowned Spitfire test pilot Jeffrey Quill and other Vickers test pilots displayed it regularly, until the company donated it to the Battle of Britain Flight in 1965. Jeffrey Quill delivered the aircraft to the Flight's RAF Coltishall base personally, his last ever flight in a Spitfire.

As Good As New

In BBMF service, AB910 has suffered damage in four flying-related incidents. Undercarriage failures in 1972 and 1976 saw it tip onto its nose, but a ground collision with a Harvard at Bex, Switzerland, in 1978, was its most serious accident. During its take-off roll the Spitfire hit the taxiing Harvard, which had encroached onto the runway, heading in the opposite direction.

The Harvard was pushed back a considerable distance and the two aircraft became locked together. Fortunately there was no fire and there were no major injuries, but AB910 sustained serious damage. An informal arrangement saw a team from the Repair and Salvage Squadron at the RAF Maintenance Unit at Abingdon repair it – AB910 re-joined the BBMF three years later.

In 2004, an inner tube failure and flat tyre on landing at Coningsby tipped the aircraft on its nose again. BBMF Spitfires are now fitted with tubeless wheels and tyres to reduce the chance of a similar occurrence.

During a major refurbishment conducted over two and a half years from October 2012, AB910 was stripped down to the barest level and rebuilt to 'as new' standard, with much improved authenticity, including a three-bladed propeller. ⊙

Now with accurate exhausts and propeller, AB910 starts up as *peterjohn. 'I'* alongside the BBMF hangar at Coningsby, early in October 2015. Sgt Andy Benson/© UK MoD Crown Copyright 2017

AB910 was among relatively few Spitfire Mk VBs still on the front line in June 1944. Jim Dooley Photography

F
SH

During the 1970s, LF363 was painted to represent a Hurricane flown by Douglas Bader during the Battle of Britain. Key Collection

In 2017, LF363 abandons these 1 Sqn markings for a dual identity celebrating the careers of wartime Hurricane pilots Tom Neil and Paul Farnes. Cpl Phil Major/© UK MoD Crown Copyright 2017

Below: The view from PA474's tail turret as the BBMF, including LF363, led the flypast over Buckingham Palace for Her Majesty The Queen's Diamond Jubilee on June 5, 2012. SAC Daniel Herrick/© UK MoD Crown Copyright 2017

Hurricane Mk IIC LF363

Squadron Leader Clive Rowley MBE RAF (Retd) tells the story of BBMF's Hurricane Mk IIC LF363

Hurricane LF363 was built in the Hawker factory at Langley, near Slough, Berkshire, in the winter of 1943. Finished as a Mk IIC, it was fitted with four 20mm cannon and a Rolls-Royce Merlin XX engine. First flown on New Year's Day 1944, LF363 was initially delivered to 5 MU at Kemble, Wiltshire, on January 28.

On March 30, an Air Transport Auxiliary (ATA) ferry pilot collected LF363 from Kemble and delivered it to 63 Sqn at Turnhouse, near Edinburgh. The unit had recently given up its Allison-engined tactical reconnaissance North American Mustang Mk Is, and was now using Hurricanes as it trained for naval artillery spotting in preparation for D-Day. In early May it re-equipped with Spitfire Mk Vs and moved south to Lee-on-Solent to become part of the D-Day Air Spotting Pool.

LF363 was re-allocated to 309 (Polish) Sqn at Drem, near North Berwick, East Lothian, on May 23, 1944. Like the squadron's other Hurricanes, LF363 was modified with a camera for maritime reconnaissance. The unit's aggressive Polish pilots were deeply disappointed to be moved so far from the

Squadrons Then and Now

Number	Established	Initial Aircraft	Hurricane Service	2017 Role	Aircraft
1	April 13, 1912	Nieuport 17 (from March 1916)	Mk I October 1938-April 1941 & April-July 1942, Mk IIA February-June 1941, Mk IIB April 1941-January 1942 & June-September 1942	Air Defence & Offensive Support	Typhoon
501	June 14, 1929	DH.9A	Mk I March 1939-April 1941	Provision of Royal Auxiliary Air Force (RAuxAF) logisticians	None

Historic Flying worked miracles to restore LF363 after its crash landing at Wittering. Key Collection

D-Day action. Instead, they spent endless hours on readiness, flying patrols off Scotland's east coast and over the Firth of Forth, and on shipping protection and air defence duties, with no sign of enemy aircraft. In October 1944, 309 Sqn received a full complement of new Mustang IIIs. It was back in business and the Hurricanes, including LF363, were taken away.

Non-operational

For the remainder of the war LF363 served in non-operational roles with several units. At war's end it was with 62 OTU at Ouston. Subsequently, it was on charge at Middle Wallop and with the Fighter Command Communications Squadron at Northolt. By February 1948 it was with Thorney Island's Station Flight and apparently in a sorry state, classified as 'u/s [unserviceable] awaiting spares'.

Following repairs, the aircraft took part in the Battle of Britain flypast over London in September 1948, but suffered a forced landing soon after. It was sent to Hawker at Langley, where it sat in the open with no apparent future planned, except perhaps scrapping or being broken up for spares.

But it was saved, not least following intervention by the Air Officer Commanding (AOC) of Fighter Command's 11 Group, Air Vice-Marshal Sir Stanley Vincent CB DFC AFC. During the Battle of Britain, then Group Captain Stanley Vincent had been station commander at Northolt while Hurricanes were operating from the airfield. Vincent, who was, incidentally, the only RAF fighter pilot to score kills in both World Wars, planned to see an RAF Hurricane airworthy again before he retired.

He wanted it to become a commemoration of all that the type had achieved in World War Two, and he also harboured a dream of personally leading the annual Battle of Britain flypast over London, in a Hurricane. After LF363 was declared fit for flight in the summer of 1949, it was ferried back to Thorney Island, but the pilot could not lower the undercarriage and performed a wheels-up landing on the grass beside the runway.

Vincent remained determined that the Hurricane would be fit to fly in the Battle of Britain flypast, however, and in just six weeks of hard work by the long-suffering ground crew, it was made airworthy again. Sir Stanley Vincent led the Battle of Britain flypast over London in LF363 on September 15, 1949.

Between 1949 and 1956, LF363 was rather unofficially held and maintained by a series of frontline squadrons and Station Flights. It flew on ceremonial occasions, leading the Battle of Britain flypasts over London every year, and appeared in various films. In July 1957, after a major re-fit at Hawker, LF363 became a founding aircraft of the RAF Historic Flight at its Biggin Hill inauguration.

Airworthy Again

The Hurricane remained on strength as the Flight evolved into the Battle of Britain Memorial Flight, but then disaster struck. Flying between Coningsby and Jersey on September 11, 1991, LF363 suffered an engine mechanical failure, followed by a crash landing at RAF Wittering when the engine failed completely at a late stage in the approach to land. The aircraft was seriously damaged by the crash and a fierce fire, although the pilot fortunately escaped with only a broken ankle and minor burns.

Historic Flying re-built LF363 between 1994 and 1998, when it flew again for the first time in seven years. It re-joined the BBMF to represent an eight-machine gun Hurricane Mk IIA.

2017 Scheme

For the 2017 display season, LF363 will be painted with code letters honouring two surviving members of the Few. Like P7's new codes, they will be applied in a special temporary paint.

The starboard side 'SD-A' code was worn by P2760, a 501 Sqn Hurricane operated by Paul Farnes during the Battle of Britain. He flew it from the official start of the Battle on July 10, to September 14. The aircraft was destroyed in combat over Ashford, Kent on the 15th; its pilot that day, Belgian Pilot Officer Albert Van Den Hove d'Ertsenryck, was killed. Farnes was credited with eight 'kills' (including two shared), two 'probables' and 11 damaged. He was awarded the DFM and retired from the RAF as a wing commander.

The 'GN-F' codes to port were worn by P3616 and V7313, 249 Sqn Hurricanes flown by Tom Neil during the Battle of Britain. He completed 61 sorties in V7313 between September 1 and October 17, 1940, out of 141 missions during the Battle. Both Tom's GN-F coded Hurricanes were lost while other squadron pilots were at their controls. Tom was credited with 12 confirmed kills, plus four shared. He retired from the RAF as a wing commander with a DFC and Bar, and an AFC. ⊙

By the 1980s, the aircraft had been repainted as an 85 Sqn night fighter. Key Collection

Dakota Manning

Flying ZA947

Flight Lieutenant Tim 'Twigs' Dunlop describes flying the Dakota, from the viewpoint of his first training sortie almost a decade ago

When I joined the Flight in 2009, my instructor gave me a thorough brief prior to my first Dakota flight, some of which I'm sure was designed to scare me! Not only was I new to the team, but I'd never flown a tail-dragger – modern aircraft have a steerable nosewheel at the front, rather than a tailwheel at the back. He said the engines would require three hands to start; an engine failure after take-off was rather 'tricky' and the physical properties of a tail-dragger would tend towards a ground loop (a spin through 180°) on landing! But the Dakota was quintessentially a Hercules from an earlier era

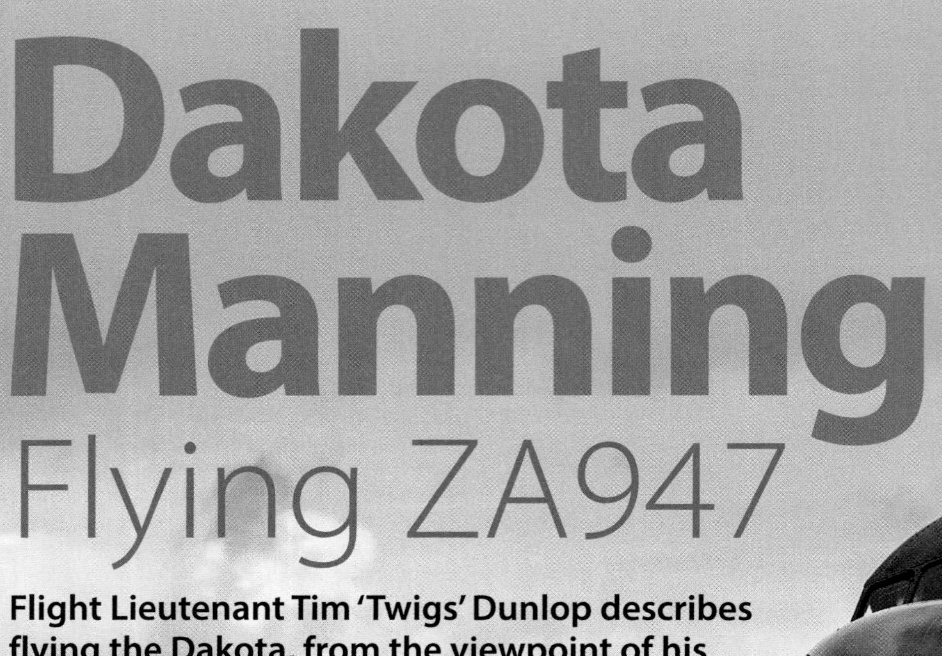

Up on the flight deck, two sets of busy hands have brought ZA947's starboard Pratt & Whitney to life. SAC Chris Ellis/© UK MoD Crown Copyright 2017

and I used to fly the Hercules, so undeterred and still rather excited to be embarking on a new career flying warbirds, I boarded ZA947 with my instructor.

I'd been on board several times before, trying to learn my checks like every good student should! The first thing I'd noticed as I made my way up to the flight deck is just how steep the freight bay floor is, a lesson I should have noted for the subsequent take-off. Through the flight deck door, the navigator station occupies the port side, although BBMF doesn't use it, our navigator sitting in the right-hand seat (RHS) pilot position; only one pilot usually flies the Dakota.

Opposite the navigator station, on the starboard side of the aircraft is an array of boxes and wires where the avionics sit. Most of the systems are as they would have been during the 1940s, but we do have a couple of modern aids, including satellite navigation. The aircraft's instruments are basic, but there's a certain comforting familiarity about everything in the cockpit.

The somewhat basic Dakota cockpit as it appeared in 2012. Today the instrument panel is black. Cpl Paul Robertshaw/© UK MoD Crown Copyright 2017

Left: The loadmaster works in the cabin, taking care of passenger safety and keeping a careful lookout from the rear cabin door and the aircraft's windows. Cpl Phil Major/© UK MoD Crown Copyright 2017

Engine Start

I settled into the left-hand seat (LHS) with my instructor beside me; a navigator would join us, but since I was under instruction and the pilots' seats were occupied, he stood in the middle behind them. A loadmaster would also be on board, responsible for the freight bay area and assisting with look out.

We ran through the checklist until we met the first hurdle, starting the engines. It truly is a two-man process, the pilot in the LHS starts the clock and calls for the RHS occupant to select 'Energise', which rotates a flywheel. At the same time, the pilot primes the engine with fuel for a couple of seconds. After 15 seconds the pilot asks for 'Mesh' to be selected, essentially engaging the flywheel to the engine through a clutch, which assists the starter motor; the propeller begins to rotate and one entire rotation ('three-blades' of the propeller) is counted.

The pilot then selects the magnetos to 'Both' (the on position) and quickly moves his right hand to the Mixture lever so he can select 'Auto Rich' as the engine catches (the mixture controls the amount of fuel entering the engine). While all this is happening, the pilot also gives the odd blip of fuel priming with his left hand, further encouraging the engine to start (it's something of a black art). Once the engine catches, the hand moves from the Mixture lever to the throttle to stop the engine over-revving and that's it! Then it's the turn of the other engine...

Taxiing

After completing the starting checks, I moved on to something I'd never considered difficult before – taxiing. The Dakota has a reasonably large tail fin, so she wants to weathercock into wind all the time – it's one of the reasons we don't like flying on windy days. So while your left hand holds the control column fully back into your stomach, moving the elevator up to apply downward pressure to the tailwheel, your right hand adjusts the throttles. »

ZA947 prepares to taxi for the runway, as crowds look on from outside the Flight's Coningsby hangar. SAC Graham Taylor/© UK MoD Crown Copyright 2017

Steering is via the upper section of the rudder pedals, which apply brakes to the individual main wheels, although asymmetric power is also used. With my hands full and the aircraft constantly trying to turn into wind, the instructor casually asked me to wave to the public on the fence line. "With what? My tongue?"

Take-off

Eventually we made it to the runway. A tailwheel lock helps keep the aircraft straight as it takes off, so I applied it and set intermediate power. The dynamics of a propeller-driven tail-dragger cause the aircraft to yaw as power is applied, to the left in the case of the Dakota, a tendency countered with right rudder. I handed the throttles over to the navigator (now kneeling between the seats), he applied full power and the aircraft accelerated down the runway.

"Push forward," the instructor commanded and I pushed the control column forward, raising the tail. I lowered the nose and selected what I thought would be a level attitude, "More!" he said, "More again!" I should have remembered how steep the climb up the freight bay was – it felt as if we were 'wheelbarrowing' down the runway. At a speed of 90kt, "Rotate!" was called and I pulled the control column back to climb the aircraft away. As we climbed, the navigator selected the undercarriage up.

At 200ft my attention turned back to the engines. Precise power settings have to be used because engine resonance resulting from incorrect settings causes fatigue and could ultimately shake the tail off – that wouldn't make for a good day! I set maximum climb power of 42in manifold air pressure (MAP) and 2,550 propeller rpm, in that order. Piston engines don't like low rpm settings with high MAP, so pilots remember the mnemonic "Rev up, power down". For more power you increase rpm before moving the throttles; for less power, you reduce the throttle setting (MAP) and then reduce the rpm.

The Dakota's climb rate at 110kt is pretty limited; I can't imagine how slowly she would have crept into the air carrying a heavy load during her operational days. To preserve the engines, a cruise climb power of 35in MAP/2,350rpm is set at 500ft. The climb rate is now roughly 500ft per minute, something that needs to be remembered while flying at low level – rising terrain can quickly out climb the aircraft!

Typically for aircraft featuring side-by-side pilot seats, the Dakota is usually flown from the left-hand seat. Cpl Phil Major/© UK MoD Crown Copyright 2017

Manoeuvring

Visual lookout is limited – the Lancaster has a large 'greenhouse' canopy, providing excellent visibility, but the Dakota has only a relatively small 'letter box' to look through. In a right-hand turn this can prove difficult for the pilot because he quite often can't see the point he's turning towards. He's therefore reliant upon the navigator and loadmaster to talk him onto the intended target.

For my first trip we climbed to about 4,000ft so I could get used to handling the aircraft, safely away from the ground. I selected a cruise power setting of 29in MAP and 2,050rpm, with the mixture settings reduced to Auto Lean; Auto Rich is required for the higher power settings, but this makes the aircraft quite thirsty on fuel. We settled at around 130kt, our regular transit speed.

Turning the Dakota really teaches you to use the rudder. Modern aircraft roll quite easily with the use of ailerons alone, but you need to 'lead with rudder' to help the Dakota turn. Her roll rate is what you'd expect of a large aircraft and is not dissimilar to that of the Hercules.

On pitching up the aircraft loses speed quickly, but doesn't climb quickly, so she can take quite a while to regain lost speed. The instructor told me to carry out a couple of stalls to get a feel for the aircraft. The Dakota stalls very gently, with a small pitch-down nod of the nose. Full Power is then selected to recover, remembering to set the mixture and rpm.

Descent and Landing

With the stalls complete it was time to return to Coningsby. The engines cool very quickly at low power settings, so you can't descend with the throttles closed; this, coupled with a maximum speed of 169kt, means that not only does she climb slowly, but she descends slowly too. For the circuit the mixture is selected to Auto Rich, with 2,350rpm and roughly 25in MAP, but this depends on the weight of the aircraft and the outside temperature.

After the instructor had given me a demonstration of the circuit and a landing, it was my turn. The navigator lowered the undercarriage using a combination of levers, moving a locking pin and directing hydraulic fluid into the 'down' line. Flap is lowered through an on/off control valve, the navigator opening the valve to let the flap travel and closing it to stop further movement. 'Flap 1' is selected and a set of checks carried out downwind. Now for the difficult bit!

At the end of the downwind leg, the throttles are retarded to approximately 17in MAP and as the speed decreases through 97kt, 'Flap 2' is selected. The aircraft descends and is turned towards the runway, aiming to roll out on the centreline at about 200ft. The approach angle is shallower than on a modern aircraft, since a steeper approach could lead to an interesting bounce, although that seems to happen on the odd occasion anyway!

The aircraft must be kept flying straight as you touchdown, so the wing-down technique is required for anything other than a wind straight down the runway. Any crosswind requires the aircraft to be kicked straight using rudder, then aileron is used to bank into wind, stopping any drift and flying the aircraft down slightly cross-controlled. Speed is reduced to 80kt before the throttles are smoothly closed and the control column 'checked back' to flare.

There was a 'squeak' as the upwind main wheel gently landed-on (beginners luck), but the aircraft wasn't safely landed yet. Aileron was used to roll us level, lowering the other main wheel onto the runway, and the aircraft began to decelerate. The flaps are selected 'up' to reduce remaining lift, but as the tail lowers the aircraft body 'blanks' the slipstream effect on the tail, reducing its effectiveness; for a moment the aircraft feels as if it is going to depart off the side of the runway. Then the tailwheel touches and, thanks to the lock, the Dakota feels stable again.

All that was left was to disengage the tailwheel lock (at slow speed) and taxi back. The lock is easy to forget until it's time to turn off the runway and the Dakota continues on in a straight line; this can be embarrassing if you're approaching the end of the runway…

Dakota Display

The BBMF Dakota display is designed to show the aircraft off gracefully and at her best. It follows a similar pattern to the Lancaster routine, reducing how much the BBMF bomber pilots need to remember! The display lasts approximately five minutes and is quite physical as we work to get the aircraft rolling quickly enough to keep it in front of the crowd. At the start of the season you certainly feel it in your shoulders after a couple of display work-up sorties in one day. The Dakota's speed precludes us from displaying with the Spitfire and Hurricane – we'd be at full speed while the fighters would be a bit too slow; it's not a good mix.

The Dakota frequently dropped paratroops during its operational career and today we drop the RAF Falcons and other teams, their members free falling from the aircraft and pulling ripcords to deploy their parachutes. But when the Dakota is used on commemorative paratroop drops, such as that at Arnhem, a static line system is used. The parachute ripcord is essentially attached to the aircraft, so it's automatically pulled when the parachutist jumps – it's the same method used during the mass drops of World War Two.

The Dakota is quite stable during these drops, with 'Flap 1' enabling a lower dispatch speed (90kt), minimising the 'shock' of the airflow as the parachutists leave the aircraft. It's quite a sight to see 'Paras', dressed in 1940s' kit, jumping onto the Arnhem dispatch zone, followed by several C-130s also dropping paratroopers.

After eight years with BBMF, I don't find the Dakota's engines any easier to start, it's still challenging to taxi and the landings require my utmost concentration, but I wouldn't change it for anything! ⊙

Dakota crews have to maintain constant concentration, even during the final stage of taxiing in. Coningsby is a busy station that works hard to accommodate the Flight, as the resident Typhoons and Sentry – temporarily based at Coningsby while Waddington's runway was rebuilt – show. Cpl Phil Major/© UK MoD Crown Copyright 2017

Battle of Britain Summer

In 2015, BBMF marked the 75th anniversary of the Battle of Britain. Flight Lieutenant Antony 'Parky' Parkinson MBE recalls: "All of us, especially the fighter pilots, had an exceptionally busy and unforgettable summer." Here he looks back at just a few of those extraordinary days

Historians have chosen July 10, 1940 as the official start of the Battle of Britain. The Luftwaffe had amassed thousands of aircraft in France and began the campaign with bombing attacks against British convoys in the English Channel, as well as ports and towns in Southeast England. The German intention was to achieve complete air superiority as a prerequisite to invasion. The greatest air battle ever had begun; the survival of our nation hung in the balance.

75 Years Later

I'm strapped into Spitfire Mk XVI TE311 and check my watch. It's the morning of July 10, 2015 and it's turning out to be a beautiful day, in contrast to the cloudy, showery conditions of 75 years ago. Check-in on the radio is in three minutes and the other BBMF Spitfires and Hurricanes glint in the sunshine around me.

A BBC Breakfast TV crew is filming a live piece to camera next to my Spitfire and the presenter, Danny Savage, asks me if I'd be happy to say a few words. I briefly tell him what we're about to do and try my best to convey how unbelievably privileged I feel to be a part of this special formation flypast over Buckingham Palace. Not only will the Royal Family be on the balcony today, but also some of the 'Few' will be in attendance.

The Merlins roar to life and soon four Spitfires and two Hurricanes are streaming down Coningsby's westerly runway and into the air. We join up for a six-ship flypast over the hundreds of visitors who have cheered and waved us off. The sight of so many fighters in the air around me has the hair standing up on the back of my neck and I know that my fellow pilots are also soaking up this special moment.

We roar over North Weald, a Battle of Britain airfield just to the north east of London, and break into the circuit to land. The flying club is packed with excited faces and our groundcrew arrive bang on time, ready to refuel and prepare the fighters for the big event.

Buckingham Palace

London looks stunning. Squadron Leader Dunc Mason, OC BBMF, leads the five-ship over the Palace to the second and, flying outside on the right, I have a fantastic view of our formation as the River Thames, the London Eye and the Houses of Parliament flash by in my peripheral vision. Behind us, Wing Commander Justin Helliwell, in another of the BBMF Spitfires, leads a Eurofighter Typhoon, followed by a final three-ship of Typhoons.

Then it's back to North Weald and smiles all round as the boys check the internet for pictures of the formation. We stumble across a photo of Squadron Leader Geoffrey Wellum DFC, among the youngest of the 'Few', looking up at the flypast from The Mall, with a beaming smile on his face.

Special Tributes

In November 2014, at a meeting with Air Officer Commanding (AOC) 1 Group, OC BBMF

Synchro 75's Typhoon was painted to represent the 249 Sqn Hurricane flown by Flt Lt James Nicolson on August 16, 1940. After combat with a Junkers Ju 88 and Bf 109 fighters had left him wounded and his aircraft burning, Nicolson engaged a Bf 110 before baling out. He was awarded the Victoria Cross for his actions. BAE Systems

"... Ben would hold close formation through the various manoeuvres."

Thanks to a little digital magic, Parky's Spitfire appeared in Coningsby's Typhoon simulator! © UK MoD Crown Copyright 2017

and I discussed the options we proposed to ensure we marked the 75th anniversary of the Battle of Britain with a fitting tribute.

Our first decision was to fly the Spitfire and Typhoon 'Synchro 75' display. This had previously been flown in 2010 to mark the 70th anniversary and was exceptionally well received at airshows. The simple act of flying the Spitfire and Typhoon in formation – both of them representing the cutting edge technology of their time – and then executing a dynamic synchronised display, where the two aircraft perform opposition passes and turns, was a winning formula. This time, though, a Typhoon would be painted in full Battle of Britain colours, making the Synchro 75 even more special.

BBMF traditionally flies the Synchro with either two Spitfires or a Spitfire and Hurricane, so we weren't selling something entirely radical to the AOC and having done it before we knew it would work with a Typhoon.

We also agreed to fly a formation of BBMF Spitfires and Hurricanes with The Royal Air Force Aerobatic Team The Red Arrows, and to lead a number of balbos (large formations) of World War Two fighters in co-operation with our civilian counterparts and led by OC BBMF. »

Three BBMF Spitfires and both Hurricanes overfly Buckingham Palace to mark the 75th anniversary of the Battle of Britain on July 10, 2015. © UK MoD Crown Copyright 2017

With P7350 a little reluctant to begin the 2015 season, Spitfire Mk V AB910 and Hurricane LF363 occasionally stood in for Synchro 75 purposes. Cpl Phil Major/© UK MoD Crown Copyright 2017

Dunc Mason led the BBMF fighter formation in a series of beautifully executed passes over IWM Duxford for its Battle of Britain Airshow on September 20. After the final pass, the aircraft departed to return a few minutes later, after joining up with...

... The Royal Air Force Aerobatic Team The Red Arrows. Both Paul E Eden

Above: Tom Neil (left, who flew Hurricanes with 249 Sqn) and Geoffrey Wellum (Spitfires, 92 Sqn) were among the veterans watching the July 10 flypast in London. © UK MoD Crown Copyright 2017

Synchro 75

Since Dunc Mason was leading the balbos, he chose me to fly the Synchro 75 Spitfire. Flight Lieutenant Ben Westoby-Brooks, a mate of mine from Typhoon days and now a Qualified Pilot Instructor with 29(R) Squadron, would fly the Typhoon.

With its computing power and lifelike graphics, Ben and I used Coningsby's Typhoon simulator to good effect to prepare and perfect the Synchro 75 routine prior to Public Display Approval (PDA). Thanks to the simulator 'visuals', we could practise at any venue, in any conditions and, although I was flying another Typhoon simulator, when Ben looked out from his cockpit, he saw a Spitfire! It obviously helped that I was experienced in flying the Typhoon.

For the first three minutes of the display I would essentially be flying my fairly gentle, solo Spitfire routine and Ben would hold close formation through the various manoeuvres. Then we would run in, pointing at the crowd, for a Synchro break before 'mirroring' each other, flying crosses and opposition 360° turns.

The wind plays a big part in any Synchro display, with one of you always extending to allow for the wind. But because Ben could actually set the Typhoon to maintain an exact speed, he could match the Spitfire's parameters. The speeds at which Ben would be flying, in the 200 to 250kt regime, are no problem for the Typhoon's carefree handling and, while it's a little slow, the aircraft is very happy to fly at these speeds. We knew it was a proven display, so it was really just a question of practising, making sure the 'crosses were in the middle' and the 'fudges' to adjust for the wind looked good. The work-up and PDA went well and the AOC approved the display.

We flew our first public Spit/Typhoon Synchro 75 display at Abingdon in early May. However P7350, our beautiful Spitfire Mk IIA (the only surviving airworthy Battle of Britain Spitfire) was unserviceable for Abingdon. So we hatched a plot to fly both the BBMF formation with the Red Arrows and Synchro 75 with P7350 at Biggin Hill in June. It was our first chance to fly the matching Spitfire and Typhoon schemes in public.

Biggin Hill

Saturday, June 13, 2015 and Biggin Hill, a famous Battle of Britain airfield, is holding a

The Synchro 75 routine featured spectacular opposition work.
BAE Systems

Now for the Synchro part of the display and I roll out, pointing directly at the crowd, with Ben tucked in behind. "Synchro, Break, Break, Go!" And we're off. I go left. Ben goes right. We pull up into a Derry wingover (rolling through 270°), adjust for the wind and now we're pointing towards one another.

We cross near enough at the middle of the crowd line as the Typhoon goes flashing past. More opposition passes follow and then we position for the final pass. "Pull!" I call as I pull up into a victory roll while Ben selects full reheat and comes rocketing past me, up into an almost vertical climb. It's over. Again I feel a huge sense of privilege to have been allowed to fly this display in this historic year.

Steedman Display Sword

Ben and Parky's Synchro 75 received plaudits from the public and professional aviators alike. At the Royal International Air Tattoo in July 2015, the display's excellence was recognised with the award of the Steedman Display Sword for the Best Flying Demonstration by a UK participant.

Parky's name was already on the trophy – he won it in 2000 as the Tornado F3 display pilot. Now he features twice, in two very different aircraft!

very special airshow. The excitement builds as three BBMF Spitfires and two Hurricanes hold over Sevenoaks. We're watching the Red Arrows complete their display and then route towards us, slowing as they do so.

The join-up is made difficult by a tight run into Biggin Hill owing to Gatwick's airspace, but Dunc leads it perfectly and the five BBMF fighters slot into position behind the 'Reds'. Again I'm on the outside right of the fighters, but this time my peripheral vision is filled with red Hawks. I glance up and to my right for an excellent view up Red 8's jet pipe! We fly through Biggin Hill and can almost sense rather than see the huge crowd. We back off, allowing the 'Reds' to land before Dunc positions our five-ship for more passes over the airfield.

After the last pass, I break out of formation and check to see if Ben is on frequency in the Typhoon. He is, and holding for me. I position 'crowd rear' and Ben joins the beautifully painted Typhoon a few feet away on my right wing. I look out over my Spitfire's elliptical wing to a remarkably close and surprisingly large Typhoon, painted to match my aircraft – what a view!

But there's no time to dwell on it as we position for run in to our 'topside'-bend arrival. I call Ben into line astern formation and can see from the shadow over the Kent fields that he's positioned perfectly as we fly a 360° turn in front of the crowd.

The Few

The 'Few' inevitably become fewer, but it's the veterans we meet and feel honoured to call our mates that are the utmost highlight of the BBMF job.

There's one memory I hope will remain with me forever. It was late and I walked into the quiet bar of a large hotel in Ashford, Kent. Battle of Britain fighter pilot Geoffrey Wellum was sitting at the bar, sipping a pint of ale. He'd quietly removed himself from a formal dinner. He looked up and his face once again lit up. Along with my fellow BBMF fighter pilots, we laughed and chatted about the events of 75 years before. Later, as we left, he said to me, "Safe landings old boy". ⊙

Parky leads Ben in BBMF's genuine Battle of Britain Spitfire.
BAE Systems

"Synchro, Break, Break, Go!" And we're off. I go left. Ben goes right."

Spitfire Superlative

Considerably more ambitious in design than Hawker's Hurricane, the Spitfire exhibited extraordinary development potential. While the Hurricane was exactly the fighter the RAF needed in summer 1940, the Spitfire was the machine it needed for the rest of the war

The Spitfire Mk VB was ubiquitous in RAF service. Among its many operators, 234 Sqn flew the type in the summer of 1942. All Key Collection

On September 12, 1931, Flight Lieutenant Boothman flew Supermarine S.6B S1595 to victory in the Schneider Trophy Contest. The competition rules stated that any nation taking three consecutive wins would claim the trophy for all time, and since the 1929 event had gone to the S.6 and the 1927 race to the S.5, Boothman's win made Great Britain the outright winner.

Designer Reginald J Mitchell had been responsible for the S.5 and S.6 designs, and their S.4 predecessor. He'd also penned a series of successful Supermarine seaplanes and schemes for various other aircraft, including the uninspiring Type 224 fighter prototype designed in response to Air Ministry specification F.7/30.

Like Sydney Camm at Hawker, Mitchell was hamstrung by the Ministry's faith in the ill-fated Goshawk engine, provision for which compromised his prototype. But concerned at developments on the Continent and convinced of the RAF's need for modern fighter aircraft, he continued with the development of a new fighter infinitely superior to the clumsy Type 224.

Drawing inspiration from his racing aeroplanes, Mitchell concentrated on creating an aerodynamically 'clean' design for maximum performance. He chose all-metal, stressed skin construction, a thoroughly modern technique that distributed flight loads across the airframe rather than along particular paths. The result further contributed to the fighter's performance, although there was relatively little experience of building or maintaining stressed skin aircraft, especially within the RAF, and the machine's development and service entry were consequently somewhat more protracted than those of the Hurricane.

Lightweight Browning

By now, Air Ministry trials had informed selection of the 0.3in Colt machine gun to replace the ancient 0.303in Vickers as the standard fighter armament. Modified to 0.303in to suit British ammunition and built as the Browning, the new weapon was lighter and smaller than the Vickers and in specification F.5/34 the Air Ministry called for a fighter armed with eight of the new weapons.

Bristol, Gloster, Martin-Baker and Vickers all submitted designs against F.5/34, but Hawker and Supermarine already had high-speed monoplane fighters in hand, both recently buoyed by Rolls-Royce's promising Merlin. Camm and Mitchell had already realised the eight-gun requirement and created their designs accordingly, so that F.5/34 was replaced by specifications written specifically around the private venture machines, the Hurricane and what would soon become the Spitfire.

Known by the company designation Type 300, the Supermarine design featured a thin, »

The Spitfire's wings were often clipped for the low-level role, removal of the elliptical tips improving role rate. This is a Mk VC.

High And Low Specialists

Two Spitfire fighter variants were developed to counter Luftwaffe aircraft flying high-altitude bombing and reconnaissance missions over Great Britain. Both types featured pressurised cockpits and engines adapted for high-altitude operations.

The Mk VI flew first, in June 1941, powered by the 1,415hp Merlin 47 engine. Entering service with 616 Sqn in April 1942, the variant scored its premier kill, a Dornier Do 217, on May 25.

Flown for the first time in April 1942, the Spitfire Mk VII introduced the 1,520hp Merlin 61 into service. Like the Mk VI, the Mk VII featured extended wing tips for better high-altitude handling, but also employed the retractable tailwheel and pointed rudder used on the Mk VIII.

In service from September 1942, the Mk VII's victories included an Fw 190 downed at 38,000ft over Plymouth. Sixteen Mk VIIs were later converted as high-level PR aircraft, designated Spitfire PR.Mk X. In addition, 26 Spitfire PR.Mk XIII aircraft were produced specifically for low-altitude reconnaissance, through the conversion of Mk V airframes.

elliptical wing, again for optimal performance, although it was trickier to manufacture even that the Hurricane's metal wing. It also had limited space for machine guns and while the thick-winged Hawker featured two bays each holding four guns, the Spitfire's weapons were spaced out along the wing – in operational terms it dictated that the Hurricane could be quickly rearmed through simple panels on the upper wing, while the Spitfire required armourers to work more slowly from below, through drop-down panels, looking upwards into the wing.

The Type 300's predicted performance led the Air Ministry to write F.37/34 around it and the prototype finally became airborne on March 5, 1936. Early in July, the first contract – for 310 Spitfires, as the aircraft had by then been named – was placed, with the aim of having aircraft in service by March 1939.

In the event, a change from Merlin I to Merlin II for initial Hurricane and Spitfire production caused delays in both programmes for limited redesign work, but the Spitfire subsequently required rather more fettling to get right in other aspects of its performance. It also suffered problems with its gun installations, which were prone to icing, and with windscreen misting during descent from altitude. Both issues continued to plague the type long after the first Spitfire Mk I was delivered to 19 Sqn on August 4, 1938 and neither it, nor 66 Sqn, the second Spitfire operator, was fully operational until 1939.

When the RAF deployed fighters to support the British Expeditionary Force despatched to France from September 1939, it sent Gladiators and Hurricanes, judging the Spitfire too immature for combat abroad. The type's gun and windscreen problems were ongoing, the Service was still struggling to come to grips with its maintenance and repair requirements, and its narrow track undercarriage was considered less suitable for typically bumpy French airfields than the Hurricane's wide track arrangement.

Fighter Supreme

Flying from better prepared airfields at home, however, the Spitfire began to show its mettle. On October 16, 1939, No. 602 'City of Glasgow' Sqn downed a pair of Junkers Ju 88s over the Firth of Forth, while 603 'City of Edinburgh' Sqn shot a KG 26 Heinkel He 111 down into the North Sea, the units thus notching up the first aerial victories over Great Britain since World War One.

On the 28th, the squadrons combined forces to bring another KG 26 He 111 down; this time the enemy machine crashed on land, in the Lammermoor Hills, close to Dalkeith, becoming the first enemy aircraft of the conflict shot down onto British soil. Meanwhile, Supermarine continued ramping up production so that by July 1940, 14 Spitfire squadrons were at full strength, with five more working up, compared to 25 and four, respectively, on the Hurricane.

In the momentous events that followed, the Spitfire matched and frequently surpassed the Messerschmitt Bf 109E, the finest of Germany's

P7508 was from a batch of 1,000 Spitfires ordered as Mk IIs. Like BBMF's P7350, which comes from the same order, this aircraft was built as one of 750 Mk IIAs. The remainder of the run was completed as 170 cannon-armed Mk IIBs and 80 Mk VBs.

contemporary fighters. The Hurricane also scored its share of 'Emil' kills, but proved better suited against bombers and the less manoeuvrable Bf 110. By the end of the campaign it was clear that the Spitfire was the future of RAF air-to-air strength, while the Hurricane was destined for a second, exceptional career as a fighter-bomber.

During the Battle of Britain, the Merlin XII-engined Spitfire Mk II had begun replacing the Mk I, while the Mk IIB took 20mm cannon into battle for the first time, albeit with limited success. But the up-armed Mk IIB was a harbinger of greater things to come. With yet more power from the Merlin 45, the Spitfire Mk V was delivered from February 1941, initially as the eight-gun Mk VA. Then the Mk VB replaced four of the Brownings with two Hispano cannon, and introduced provision for bombs and auxiliary fuel tanks.

The Spitfire was now bearing the brunt of offensive operations into Europe and increasingly sent overseas, the Mk VC arriving with a modified wing capable of housing the 'A' armament of eight machine guns, the 'B' arrangement of machine gun and cannon, or a new 'C' configuration of four cannon. Both the Mk VB and C were tropicalised for service in North Africa and further afield, and their wing tips were often 'clipped', a straight device replacing the elegant elliptical tip for increased roll rate at low level.

With its moderate range addressed through the removal of all armament, the Spitfire also became an exceptional high-speed photo-reconnaissance (PR) aircraft. A complicated »

Supermarine developed the Spitfire Mk IX in response to the Focke-Wulf Fw 190. The experimental application of floats to a handful of aircraft did little for the Mk IX's performance however, and the concept was abandoned.

In the Mk VIII, Supermarine achieved the perfect balance between airframe and Merlin. Almost the entire Mk VIII production run was used overseas.

Among the ultimate Spitfires, the Mk 21 entered service just as the war was ending.

Squadrons Then and Now

Number	Established	Initial Aircraft	Spitfire Service	2017 Role	Aircraft
1	April 13, 1912	Nieuport 17 (from March 1916)	April 1944-October 1946	Air Defence & Offensive Support	Typhoon
60	April 30, 1916	Morane Scout	1946-1951	Rotary Wing Flying Training	Griffin HT1

series of modified Mk I airframes flew PR missions over occupied Europe and Germany from November 18, 1939 and was eventually surpassed by the exceptional PR.Mk XI. Entering service in 1942, the Mk XI gathered much of the intelligence vital to the D-Day landings and although the even more capable Mk XIX entered service in June 1944, the earlier machine remained in action until war's end.

Continuous Development

It is typical of the Spitfire's rapid and somewhat confusing development that the PR.Mk XI was based on the Mk VIII, a fighter and fighter-bomber variant re-engineered to make maximum utility of the 60-series Merlin. Delivering in excess of 1,700hp depending on variant, the latest Merlin was seen as the means by which the Spitfire could take on and beat the Focke-Wulf Fw 190A.

The new Luftwaffe fighter easily outclassed the Spitfire Mk V and though the Mk VIII would clearly emerge the superior aircraft, such was the urgency of the requirement that just as Mk II airframes had been rebuilt as Mk Vs, so a variety of Mk Vs was rebuilt or completed with 60-series Merlins as the Spitfire Mk IX. Considered a stopgap measure, the Mk IX was actually built to the extent of 5,656 examples, less than 1,000 fewer than the Mk V, making it the second most widespread variant. It even spawned a variant of its own, the Mk XVI, with a Packard-built Merlin 266 engine.

When the Spitfire Mk VIII finally emerged, it was as a near perfect harmonisation of airframe and engine. The Mk IX was satisfying requirements in the West, however, so by far the majority of Mk VIIIs went to squadrons in Italy (from June 1943), the Desert Air Force and Burma (from January 1944).

The Spitfire airframe/Merlin engine combination had effectively evolved in parallel, so the origins of the 405mph Mk XVI and its 1,720hp Packard Merlin 266 could be traced directly back to the 355mph Mk I and 1,030hp Merlin II. Yet there was still more to be extracted from the aircraft and the even more powerful Rolls-Royce Griffon was the engine to power the ultimate Spitfire iterations.

First to emerge, in February 1943, the Spitfire Mk XII was essentially a Mk V/IX airframe powered by the 1,735hp Griffon III or IV. Optimised for low-level work, it was tasked against fast, low-flying Fw 190 fighter-bombers attacking targets in southern England.

Next, the Spitfire Mk XIV paired the 2,050hp Griffon 65 with the Mk XIII airframe, producing a far better harmonised aircraft. Power was delivered through a five-bladed propeller, a 'universal wing' offering considerable flexibility in weaponry was introduced on the Mk XIVE and a fighter-reconnaissance variant was built as the FR.Mk XIVE. Like the Mk XVI, the Mk XIV was also built as standard with a cut-down rear fuselage and 'bubble' cockpit canopy.

The Mk XVIII, built as the F.Mk XVIII or FR.Mk XVIII (F.Mk 18 and FR.Mk 18 from 1948) featured increased fuel tankage and, in some aircraft, the 2,340hp Griffon 67. Entering service

The Spitfire made a superlative photo-reconnaissance platform, exemplified by the PR.Mk XI.

Re-engining the Spitfire with the even more powerful Griffon created a beast very different in character to the Merlin-powered machines. This is an F.Mk XIV.

in 1946, the Mk 18 flew the last operational RAF Spitfire fighter sorties, over Malaya, in January 1951.

Further operational fighter marks were also produced, however, introducing a new wing and other structural enhancements. The F.Mk 21 (confusingly, Roman numerals were used infrequently for higher-numbered marks, even before 1948) entered service early in 1945, Nos 1 and 91 Sqns briefly using it operationally. Delivered from 1947, the F.Mk 22 replaced the Mk 21's Griffon 65 with the similarly rated Griffon 85 and featured the cut-down rear fuselage.

While the Mk 22 primarily equipped Royal Auxiliary Air Force squadrons, the F.Mk 24, last of the fighter Spitfire variants, was used exclusively overseas. The last of the type was retired from 80 Sqn's ranks, in Hong Kong, during December 1951.

Operational Conclusion

The RAF's operational association with the Spitfire ended over the Malayan jungle during Operation Firedog, but not with 60 Sqn's Mk 18 fighter-bomber sorties in 1951. Powered by the 2,050hp Griffon 64 or 66, the PR.Mk 19 was also operational over Malaya, where 81 Sqn flew its final frontline sortie on April 1, 1954. The type then continued in second-line service until June 1957.

So ended the Spitfire's 19-year operational RAF career. Almost 18,300 Merlin-engined Spitfires were built, plus 2,042 Griffon-engined machines. These totals excluded the Fleet Air Arm's Seafire variants, which were also built with both engine types. During its astoundingly rapid evolution the Spitfire demonstrated unprecedented development potential, such that the F.Mk 24 of 1948 did little more than resemble the Type 300 of 1936.

The Spitfire is even better represented than the Hurricane in museum collections and airshow visitors are blessed with a splendid variety of events at which to see a 'Spit' fly. Among several airworthy Spitfires in the UK, BBMF's fleet nicely represents the type through its development, ranging from the early Mk II, through V and IX, to the Mk XVI and the Griffon-engined Mk 19. ⊙

After its service as a flying test bed with the College of Aeronautics at Cranfield ended in late 1963, Avro Lancaster BI PA474 was flown to 15 MU at Wroughton in April 1964. For very many of the Lancasters that ended up at Wroughton, the word 'Maintenance' in 15 MU's title was a misnomer, since it was actually something of a graveyard for the aircraft. The majority of those that arrived were broken up and scrapped.

But the Air Historical Branch (AHB) of the Ministry of Defence (MoD) had adopted PA474 for planned inclusion in the proposed RAF Museum, granting it a reprise from scrapping. On September 25, 1964, PA474 was therefore flown from Wroughton to the grass airfield at RAF Henlow, Bedfordshire. Henlow was a storage site for aircraft destined for the museum, which at the time was little more than a paper project. The station's hangars were of World War One vintage and their structure precluded the storage of the 102ft-span Lancaster, which was left on the grass outside, were it suffered the depredations of the weather and became a nesting site for a variety of birds. With its condition deteriorating, PA474's future lay in the balance.

D'Arcy's Quest

In 1965, No. 44 Squadron was flying the Avro Vulcan from RAF Waddington. Its commanding officer, Wing Commander Mike D'Arcy, decided that he would like to obtain a Lancaster for the squadron and the station. His squadron had been the first operational Bomber Command Lancaster unit, taking delivery of the first frontline examples, at Waddington, on Christmas Eve 1941.

Squadron Leader Leach (right) provides a radio interview after landing back at Waddington. He subsequently served with the BBMF, flying in PA474 between 1974 and 1978.

Hopes of finding a Lancaster had almost faded when the 44 Sqn team realised the existence of PA474 at Henlow. They discovered the Lancaster's AHB ownership and the museum plan, also gaining confirmation that the museum was many years away.

D'Arcy therefore approached the AHB and requested that PA474 be transferred to the care of 44 Sqn at Waddington, pointing out that it could, at least, be placed under cover in a hangar so that a degree of restoration could begin.

One Flight Only

Eventually, approval for the Lancaster's transfer was obtained and a party of ground crew from Waddington, some of whom had worked on Lancasters during the war or subsequently with Coastal Command, was sent to Henlow to conduct an airframe survey. The intention was to discover how badly corroded the Lancaster was and assess how difficult it would be to dismantle and transport by road to Waddington.

Surprisingly, the aircraft was found to be in a remarkably good state of preservation. The engines had been properly inhibited after its last flight and there appeared to be little wrong with them. Similarly, the airframe and flying controls were in good condition. The idea began to take shape that without too much effort it might be possible to fly the Lancaster to Waddington. Closer inspection revealed that work would be necessary on the electrical, hydraulic and fuel systems, but there were no identified problems that could not be solved relatively easily.

PA474 at Henlow, on the morning of August 18, 1965, with all engines running.
All via Ray Leach unless otherwise noted

Saving PA474

A request was made to the AHB for permission to fly the Lancaster to Waddington, rather than dismantle it at Henlow and transport it by RAF 'Queen Mary' low-loaders for subsequent reassembly. After considerable deliberation at high levels, authority was eventually granted for 'ONE FLIGHT ONLY' from Henlow to Waddington 'AVOIDING ALL BUILT UP AREAS'.

An enthusiastic team of volunteers serviced PA474 at Henlow over a period of weeks, mostly at weekends. After many minor problems had been overcome, the aircraft was almost ready to fly when it was discovered that the tailwheel assembly was cracked. Not wishing to bother the AHB or museum staff at Henlow with such a potentially 'show stopping' problem, the 44 Sqn team decided to solve it on a self-help basis.

Avro Lincoln RF398 was parked on the grass beside PA474 and close inspection revealed that, although different, the Lancaster and Lincoln tailwheel assemblies were interchangeable. So it was that a casual passer-by one lunchtime might have been surprised to see the two four-engined bombers with their tails propped on concrete blocks while figures scurried back and forth between them. By the end of that lunch break both aircraft were back in their normal attitudes, with only a few people to the wise. (PA474 flew with the Lincoln's tailwheel for many years.)

The Flight

With the necessary work complete, it was decided that the date of the flight would be August 18, 1965. Ray Leach explains how the move worked: "I arrived at RAF Henlow the day before the proposed flight, in company with the servicing party. My job was to liaise between RAF Waddington and the press and television teams who would be covering the flight. Following this, if all went well, I was to act as the navigator for the trip.

"The rest of the flight crew, pilot Flight Lieutenant Waclaw 'Nick' Niezreckie, flight engineer Hugh Reid (an MoD employee and ex-wartime Lancaster flight engineer) and Flying Officer M Steward, who was to act as ballast in the rear turret to keep the tail down in the early stages of the take-off run, arrived in an Avro Anson during the morning of the 18th.

"At 10:30hrs, after a thorough external check, we boarded the Lancaster and carried out the pre-flight checks. All went well until the No. 4 Fuel Low Pressure warning light illuminated. For a moment or two it looked as if all our plans would come to nothing, but after following the standard corrective procedures for such an eventuality the pilot, a man of thousands of hours of experience, decided to isolate all fuel systems except the apparently faulty one to see if it was simply an indication fault. The result was that with everything else isolated, all four engines continued to run sweetly. Turning to the flight engineer, the pilot told him to 'Take the ******* bulb out'! So, with all warning lights out, we called Henlow tower for permission to taxi.

"Earlier in the day, the station commander at RAF Henlow had briefed us on local air traffic procedures and airfield peculiarities. He ended his brief with, 'I don't care which way you take off, that's up to you, but I don't want that antique taking off over my station. You can go any other way you like, but not, repeat not, over the camp.' »

As PA474 flew over Waddington, the opportunity was taken to recreate a famous wartime 44 Sqn image featuring a Lancaster flown by Sqn Ldr David Nettleton VC.

In August 1965, Lancaster PA474 made an extraordinary flight from open air storage at RAF Henlow, to airworthy preservation at Waddington. With the permission and assistance of the flight's navigator, Squadron Leader Ray Leach MBE RAF (Retd), Squadron Leader Clive Rowley MBE RAF (Retd) tells the story

Looking rather more spruce, but still lacking nose and mid-upper turrets, PA474 is seen here with a Vulcan, later in 1965.

PA474 moved to Coltishall in 1973. It was returning there after winter servicing at St Athan in 1977 when BBMF took the opportunity for a formation with the Red Arrows, then equipped with the Folland Gnat. Key Collection

"All went well until the No. 4 Fuel Low Pressure warning light illuminated. For a moment or two it looked as if all our plans would come to nothing..."

Squadron Leader Ray Leach MBE RAF (Retd), PA474 navigator, August 18, 1965

"With this in mind, the pilot decided to assess the grass airfield with a view to determining which would be the best way to go. The crew accompanied him in a Land Rover as he inspected the airfield and checked for potholes and any other problems or obstructions. It was decided that it would be best to taxi the Lancaster as close as we could to the southeastern boundary edge and then take off in a northwesterly direction.

"Our inspection of the proposed 'best' take-off run had shown us there were several potholes to negotiate. We attempted to assess these by driving the Land Rover over them at 50mph... the effect on driver and passengers was quite startling! The pilot decided we would have to get the Lanc off the ground as quickly as possible in order to reduce the strain on the undercarriage caused by too many severe jolts.

"We took off at 12:00hrs in what can only be described as a surprising fashion! The early part of the take-off run was uneventful, but soon after the tail came up we hit rough ground. Initially it was not too bad, but it got progressively worse as our speed built up. Eventually, the flight engineer, who'd been standing to the right of the pilot for take-off, holding the throttles open, as was normal practice in Lancasters and similar aircraft, was thrown bodily forward into the instrument panel, taking the throttle levers with him. The result of this rather drastic increase in power was a take-off achieved in a little over 500 yards!

"Once we'd recovered and disentangled the flight engineer from the instrument panel, we 'cleaned up' the aircraft and turned port for a flypast over the museum sheds. It was our way of saying thank you to our servicing team and to the two members of museum staff, Ray Lee and Norman Radcliffe, for all their help and co-operation. After a low pass over the airfield and the assembled company below, we set heading for Waddington, in company with a Vickers Varsity carrying the press and television teams.

"As we neared Waddington the Varsity left us to land so that the photographers and cameramen could position to cover our arrival. To fill in time, we flew on to Scampton, where we made two low-level fast runs down the main runway, followed the second time by a steep turn so as to fly over the then gate guardian, Lancaster R5868 'S-Sugar', a 139-op wartime Lanc, now on display at Royal Air Force Museum Hendon.

"At 13:30hrs we arrived at Waddington in dramatic fashion when Nick landed the Lancaster like the Canberras he was now more used to. The result was a five-bounce landing in front of the assembled media representatives and many hyper-critical aircrew, an error for which he subsequently apologised to the station commander, Group Captain 'Cyclops' Brown."

The 'one flight only' ruling was eventually overturned and two years later, on November 7, 1967, after considerable restoration work had been completed, PA474 flew again, on an air test piloted by Waddington Station Commander, Group Captain (later Air Vice-Marshal) Arthur Griffiths, and Squadron Leader Ken Haywood. It joined the BBMF, then based at RAF Coltishall, in November 1973. ⊙

The Lancaster performs a bouncy landing at Waddington. Paint has worn away from the fairing over the nose turret position, giving the false impression of glazing.

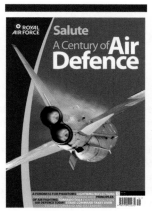

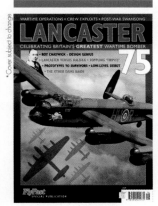

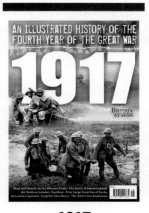

Spitfire LF.Mk IXE MK356

Squadron Leader Clive Rowley MBE RAF (Retd) tells the story of BBMF's Spitfire LF.Mk IXE MK356

Spitfire MK356 was among a batch of Mk IX Spitfires built at the Castle Bromwich factory in early 1944. Although it was equipped with full-span wing tips, the aircraft's two-speed, two-stage supercharged Rolls-Royce Merlin 66 engine was optimised for low altitudes, making the Spitfire an 'LF' (for Low-altitude Fighter) Mk IX, while its wing was of the new 'E' configuration. The aircraft was delivered to 9 MU at Cosford on February 9, 1944 for the installation of operational equipment.

On March 11, 1944, MK356 was allocated to the recently formed No. 443 ('Hornet') Squadron, RCAF, part of 144 Canadian Wing at RAF Digby (just 10 miles from the aircraft's current home at RAF Coningsby); issued to 'B' Flight, it was painted with the code letters '2I-V'. Seven days later, 144 Wing moved to Holmsley South, near Christchurch, Dorset, to be closer to the Continent for pre-invasion sorties over France.

Number 144 Wing led a nomadic life over the next couple of months, perhaps in preparation for its expeditionary role as part of the Second Tactical Air Force (2TAF) in Europe after D-Day, leapfrogging from airfield to airfield, taking MK356 with it. Hutton-Cranswick, Westhampnett (Goodwood) and the Advanced Landing Ground (ALG) at Funtingdon all hosted the Wing for brief periods, before it arrived at Ford on the Sussex coast on May 14, its base until after D-Day.

In the period leading up to the invasion and just beyond, MK356 took part in fighter and fighter-bomber operations over northern France, including tactical bomber escort and fighter-sweep missions. It flew 60 wartime sorties in 60 days, during which enemy ground fire damaged it on three occasions; a 1944 battle damage repair is still visible on MK356's rear fuselage, where a single small-arms round entered low on the starboard

Neville Duke, with Spitfire IX EN152. Finished in full desert camouflage, MK represents this aircraft for the 2017 season. Via BBMF

MK356 was previously resplendent in this all-silver scheme, representing a 601 Sqn aircraft. Paul E Eden

MK, in 443 'Hornet' Squadron markings, flies off the Lancaster's port wing in the classic BBMF three-ship formation. LA Paul A'Barrow/© UK MoD Crown Copyright 2017

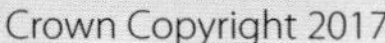

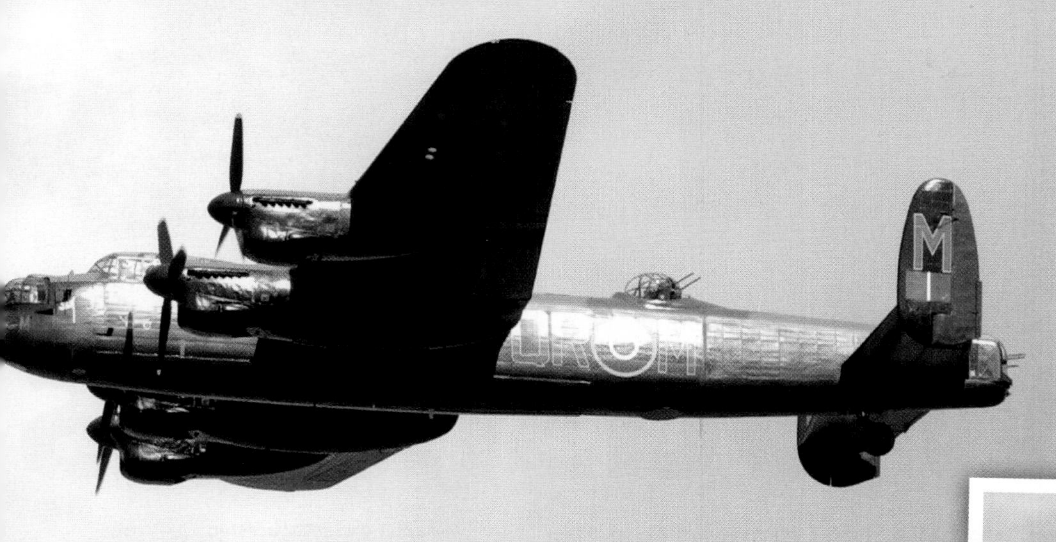

Right: In 2014, MK appeared at airshows in company with an 'invasion striped' Typhoon. The pair marked the 70th anniversary of D-Day, MK wearing an appropriate scheme representing 126 Sqn's ML214. SAC Angel Clarke/© UK MoD Crown Copyright 2017

side and exited high on the port side, just ahead of the tail. The aircraft also belly-landed twice, but was rapidly repaired and quickly back in action.

A number of 443 Sqn's pilots flew MK356, although it was regarded as the personal aircraft of 21-year old Canadian Flying Officer Gordon Ockenden DFC from Edmonton, Alberta. He flew MK356 on 19 of its 60 wartime 'ops', accumulating 40 of its total wartime flying hours of less than 100.

On D-Day, June 6, 1944, MK356 flew three beachhead cover patrols, two of them with Ockenden at the controls and each lasting approximately two hours. During another beachhead cover patrol on the afternoon of June 7 – D-Day+1 – Ockenden, flying MK356, claimed a shared kill with Flight Lieutenant Hugh Russel against a Bf 109, just off the Normandy coast.

The Spitfire flew its final wartime sortie on June 14, belly landing back at Ford after the mission because one of its main wheels had fallen off on take-off. Number 443 Sqn deployed forward to France two days later to operate from ALG B.2 at Bazenville and MK356 was left behind for collection by an MU. It did not fly again for more than 53 years.

Back to Flight

During the five decades that MK356 spent on the ground, it remained in RAF hands. It was used as a training airframe and then as a station gate guardian in the open air at Hawkinge, Bicester and Locking, where it was displayed in a flying attitude on a pole. It was used as a static airframe in the movie *Battle of Britain* in 1968, during which some overzealous picketing damaged its main spars. MK356 was then stored at Henlow, until it joined the RAF Museum's Reserve Collection at St Athan.

During the late 1980s, MK356 was surveyed with a view to its restoration to flying condition for the BBMF. Its wings were in poor condition and it was decided to use the wings of ex-Biggin Hill gate guardian Spitfire LF.Mk XVIE SL674, which had clipped tips. Work began in January 1992, a team of volunteer technicians from St Athan, led by Chief Technician Chris Bunn, carrying out the rebuild, often in their own time and with little official support.

On November 7, 1997, MK356 flew for the first time in over five decades. Flown from St Athan, this first post-restoration air test was in the capable hands of then OC BBMF, Squadron Leader Paul 'Major' Day OBE AFC. On November 14, 'The Major' delivered 'MK' to its new home with the BBMF at RAF Coningsby.

MK356 was returned to its original full-span configuration during a major servicing in 2008 and now also flies with the later, pointed, so-called 'broad chord' rudder, which increases its crosswind limits for landing.

2017 Scheme

For the 2017 season 'MK' is wearing a new desert colour scheme, representing 92 Sqn Spitfire Mk IX EN152/QJ-3 (the unit gave its Mk IX Spitfires individual numbers to differentiate them from the Mk VBs that it continued to operate alongside them). The Dark Earth (brown) and Middle Stone (sand) camouflage over Azure Blue finish makes a colourful addition to the BBMF fleet, which has not included a desert-camouflaged Spitfire in a decade.

Number 92 Sqn operated EN152/QJ-3 in Tunisia during April and May 1943. Several of the unit's pilots, including Flt Lt Neville Duke (later Sqn Ldr Duke DSO OBE DFC and two Bars AFC), flew it. A famous fighter pilot and later test pilot, Duke was the highest scoring Allied fighter ace of the Mediterranean Theatre, with 27 confirmed victories. ⊙

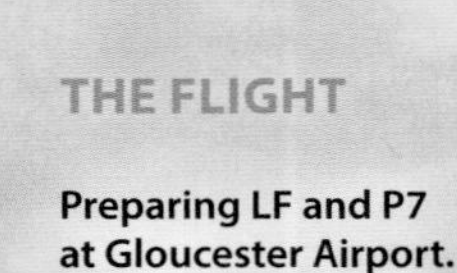

Preparing LF and P7 at Gloucester Airport.

Show Business

Watching from the ground, we take it for granted that the Battle of Britain Memorial Flight will appear on time. They'll deliver their usual immaculate display and then depart for the next venue, or land, to engage with the adoring crowds. It seems so simple, but looking back at 2016's 'RIAT weekend', Squadron Leader Mark 'Disco' Discombe reveals there's far more to it than simply turning up!

Strapping in at Gloucester, with one of the weekend's travelling ground crew.

The weekend of July 9/10 was just another in the BBMF's busy airshow schedule for 2016, but it included the Royal International Air Tattoo (RIAT) and 46 flypasts at a variety of venues. Held at RAF Fairford, Gloucestershire, RIAT is among the largest events on the airshow calendar, attracting crowds in excess of 150,000.

Spitfire and Hurricane

A month prior to the event, responsibility for the BBMF display at RIAT 2016 was allocated to me, in my second year on the Flight, as leader of a BBMF fighter pair with Wing Commander Stu Smiley, Officer Commanding Operations (OC Ops) at RAF Coningsby, who was in his first year.

The event was to have been covered by the iconic BBMF three-ship, but despite sterling work by BBMF's engineers, the Lancaster wasn't going to be available. To further complicate matters, the Dakota had also gone unserviceable and the fighters were now covering a large number of events previously planned for the 'Dak'. This meant that Wg Cdr Smiley and I had multiple other flypasts tasked at various events over the RIAT weekend. There would be lots more happening after the crowds at Fairford had waved us goodbye each day.

Disco (left) and Stu Smiley brief at Gloucester Airport over the 2016 RIAT weekend. All via BBMF

With a week to go to the event, it was time to begin planning the sorties in detail. We use the Typhoon Advanced Mission Planning Aid (TyAMPA), a computerised system with its default settings adjusted for the BBMF aircraft. This PC-based software enables us to plan sorties rapidly, save routes for other Flight members to view, edit and print. It also displays flight information warnings and 'avoids', so there's no need to check other systems or boards. But this is where the modern aids stop – in the aircraft we navigate using paper maps and a stopwatch.

The plan was to depart Coningsby on Friday afternoon and arrive into our display at Fairford. Following the display we would land and be based at Fairford for the remainder of the weekend. There were another two displays planned for RIAT, one on Saturday afternoon and another on Sunday, after which we would immediately return to Coningsby without landing. For most display crews that would be all they were expected to do, but at BBMF we plan for maximum exposure of our aircraft and we'd be completing multiple flypasts on each sortie.

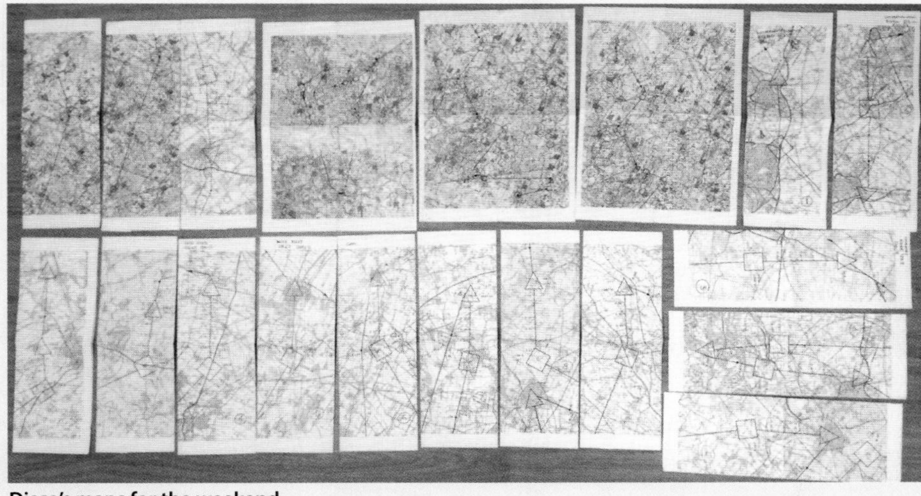

Disco's maps for the weekend.

Prior to sitting down with TyAMPA, I checked the RIAT display folder, which contained all the information sent to the Flight about the show. This allowed me to understand the timing and flow of the airshow, which aircraft were displaying before and after BBMF, and provided the mandatory display lines and other safety regulations. Then it was to business on TyAMPA, putting a simple route together for the trip down on Friday, which also had to incorporate a flypast at Burghley House, near Stamford. »

Veteran Spitfire Pilot

Part of my initial planning for the RIAT weekend, well before I considered the maps, was to organise a visit for a post-war RAF Spitfire pilot to see our aircraft. An ex-military nurse had contacted the Flight to ask whether a colleague's father, who had a distinguished post-war flying career, could meet with the BBMF at Fairford since they were planning to attend RIAT on the Saturday.

It's always a privilege to meet with pilots who have flown the aircraft we operate and the request therefore became a priority. Following a number of emails to the ex-Spitfire pilot's son and to the RIAT organisers, a plan was in place to get Flight Lieutenant John Pascoe-Watson (Retd) to the BBMF aircraft before the flying display started.

But the weather had other ideas and we were forced to operate out of Gloucester Airport rather than Fairford. After arriving at the airport on Friday and prior to setting off for our hotel, I therefore telephoned John Pascoe-Watson's son to cancel the Spitfire reunion at Fairford. Fortunately, it transpired that he lived very close to Gloucester Airport and its staff were more than happy for the veteran to visit our aircraft in their hangar on the Sunday, before we departed.

Disco and John Pascoe-Watson with P7350 at Gloucester Airport on July 10, 2016.

He told us about his experiences, gave the Flight his original Spitfire Mk XVI *Pilot's Notes* and his personal, final copy of his autobiography, both of which are now in the Flight's care. As ever, the experience reinforced the privileged position that all the Flight's aircrew and ground crew are in, reminding us of the important part we play in remembering those that have gone before and those who sacrificed so much to defend our country.

Timing would be critical to ensure we arrived just before our RIAT display slot, minimising the use of the limited hours on our aircraft. The sorties planned for Saturday and Sunday were far more complicated. Both began with a pair's display at RIAT. Following the display, the formation would split, each aircraft then covering its own individual flypasts around the country, before re-joining prior to landing. The added complication on Saturday was to return to RIAT and try to land between other displays.

Plan C

In due course we had a robust 'Plan A'. However, as all BBMF aircrew quickly learn, Plan A rarely survives for long! On Friday, as soon as we'd completed the Met (weather) brief we realised the wind was going to be an issue for the entire weekend. The BBMF imposes strict crosswind limitations on the operation of its precious historic aircraft, minimising the chances of a landing incident in these unforgiving tailwheel machines.

OC Ops, as a first-year pilot with less than 50 hours on the 'historics', was limited to a 10kt crosswind and although I was a second-year pilot with an overall 15kt limit, I was planning to take a 'baby' Spitfire. The two 'baby' Spitfires, Mk IIA P7350 and Mk VB AB910, are limited to 10kt crosswinds owing to their lightweight airframes, and small fin and rudder.

With four hours to go to departure, Plan B was to take a 15kt-crosswind Spitfire, LF.Mk XVIE TE311, enabling me to operate alone if the crosswind was between 10 and 15 kt. Then, Flt Lt Antony 'Parky' Parkinson, BBMF Ops Officer and the most experienced pilot on the Flight, had a flash of inspiration: "Why don't you operate out of Gloucester Airport? It has a south-westerly runway." Genius!

Within an hour we'd a robust Plan C, with Gloucester Airport booked for the weekend, including hangarage; all we needed to do now was re-plan all the maps and notify RIAT of our change of intentions.

Friday

As the time for the pre-flight brief approached a further concern arose – the wind at Coningsby was not abating as forecast. Following multiple phone calls and discussions, take-off was delayed. It meant we missed our Friday RIAT display slot and, therefore, our display for the day was cancelled.

Eventually, two hours later than planned, we were airborne in the Spitfire Mk IIA and Hurricane Mk IIC LF363. The sortie down to Gloucester was uneventful, with the planned Burghley House flypast en route.

After we landed at Gloucester Airport our long-suffering BBMF engineers – a team of four, led on this occasion by Flight Sergeant 'Deano' McAllister – turned up after an initial visit to Fairford, following their early morning road trip from Coningsby.

Saturday

The following morning started with the obligatory Met brief from the forecaster at RAF Coningsby, but this time over the phone during breakfast. It appeared that Parky's plan for us to relocate to Gloucester Airport was a good one, since the crosswinds at RIAT would have precluded a pair's display. Following that, the RIAT Flying Display Director (FDD) was rung to confirm that there were no last minute updates from the previous day's display brief.

Following a final check with the RIAT FDD, we took off a few minutes later than originally planned since the show was slightly behind schedule. Even so, we were held briefly to the west of Fairford before being cleared in. We ran in and completed a full pair's display.

As we departed Fairford afterwards, the real work started. We'd pre-briefed the RIAT air traffic controllers, who sit at RAF Brize Norton, of our intentions to split and follow separate routes, and they soon had us under a Traffic Service as we departed the sanctuary of the RIAT Restricted Airspace. At this point I took the Spitfire into the northern part of the Luton Air Traffic Zone for my first flypast, before routing back through Shropshire. In total I completed nine flypasts during a 1-hour 50-minute sortie.

Meanwhile, OC Ops flew south of London, up into Essex and then back west, completing a further seven flypasts on his 2-hour 10-minute sortie. We both landed back at Gloucester Airport with the absolute minimum safe fuel reserves; we'd achieved the maximum possible.

Following our epic sorties we debriefed as the engineers refuelled and prepared the aircraft for the following day. We then rang all the display and flypast venues to confirm they were happy with our performance. The last and equally challenging event of the day was to battle the RIAT road traffic to meet up with our ground support party in the RAF enclosure at Fairford. We managed a quick 'hello-goodbye', as they shut up shop for the day.

Sunday

Sunday began as Saturday had, with confirmation from the Met Office that we were at the right location to complete our task. The obligatory telephone chat with the RIAT FDD informed us that the F-35B Lightning II had blown away a display line marker at the end of Saturday's show! Then we headed to the airport for aircraft preparation and pre-flight briefings.

However, this time we had the added treat of meeting a real Spitfire pilot and talking about his exploits. Flight Lieutenant (Retd) John Pascoe-Watson was a sprightly 89-year old and he didn't need much encouragement to jump into P7350, managing the task he'd completed hundreds of times in the past with only a little help.

Afterwards, OC Ops and I completed our final plans for two more busy sorties. At this point our ground crew introduced us to Ken Farlow, a wartime RAF Spitfire engineer. He'd first met the Flight at Gloucester Airport after his daughter had posted a picture of him admiring the aircraft through the fence line. The airport manager had seen this on social media and arranged for a visit. When we returned for RIAT he paid us another visit and he was once again escorted onto the apron as a VIP. This second visit caught the imagination of the national press and the story was run in most newspapers over the following days.

Stu Smiley performs a walkaround before departure. The procedure is one of several vitally important safety checks completed before any flight.

With just enough time for a quick lunch, OC Ops and I briefed, walked to the aircraft and took-off on time. The RIAT display was completed as planned and then, once again, we split for our individual return routes to Coningsby. I took the Spitfire back to Shropshire and then south of Birmingham and up to Lincolnshire, while OC Ops flew the Hurricane via the Oxford area and then north towards home.

This time our sorties were shorter, meaning we had a little more fuel in hand to arrange our rendezvous prior to the final pair's flypast. Within a minute of each other (using only map and stopwatch) we arrived at our rendezvous point 10 miles southeast of Coningsby and joined for the final flypast just east of the base.

Following that last event we arrived over Coningsby with the usual 'hangar break' to land, then had a quick chat with the spectators watching at the fence line next to the BBMF hangar. After signing the aircraft back in, completing the ops 'paperwork' and ringing that day's event organisers, the main debrief point I had for OC Ops was a simple one: "It doesn't get much busier than that!"

The ground crew hosted former RAF engineer Ken Farlow at Gloucester airport. Sadly, Ken passed away on November 10, 2016, making his time with BBMF all the more poignant.

I stand transfixed by a silver Mk IX Spitfire, perhaps the most beloved of all marks of this most beautiful aeroplane. This must be the most divinely gorgeous and coveted machine ever built. I'm about to climb into her cockpit and we'll go flying together. Surely it's one of those fantastically realistic dreams that you believe, even after you wake?

But it's not. Having forged an entire career on astounding good luck, I continued the trend when I was selected to join the RAF Battle of Britain Memorial Flight in October 2011, which meant learning to fly piston-engined tail-draggers, a not insignificant task.

Modern tricycle undercarriages forgive a multitude of sins in landing and taxiing. But all BBMF's aircraft are tail-draggers, the only examples of their ilk remaining in the modern RAF, obliging pilots to remember myriad considerations on the ground, during take-off and on landing.

The venerable aircraft used to begin the conversion from fast jet to piston tail-dragger is the de Havilland Canada Chipmunk T.Mk 10. The flight operates two and they're in regular demand. I flew Jaguars and Typhoons for 12 years prior to joining BBMF and found it somewhat disconcerting to get into a (very) light aircraft again.

The multi-role Typhoon has 40,000lb of thrust, a maximum altitude of 55,000ft and best speed in excess of 1.5 times the speed of sound. The Chipmunk couldn't be more different, as a trainer designed in 1946 with a Gipsy Major piston engine pushing out a mere 145hp.

For all its 'mod cons', the Typhoon offers a sterile flying environment – the pilot is separated by varying degrees from the machine he commands. The control column may as well be a computer joystick, since it's not connected to the flying controls. The flaps and control surfaces are operated automatically and

Fighter Pilot Training

How does BBMF train fast jet pilots to fly Hurricanes and Spitfires? OC BBMF, Squadron Leader Andy 'Milli' Millikin, looks back at his own experience of learning to operate the Flight's fighters

Milli's fast jet background is on Jaguar and Typhoon – as here, in 2011. © UK MoD Crown Copyright 2017

"Holy cow – I was flying a Hurricane!"

seamlessly. The pilot receives no tactile feedback from the aircraft, while the control column and throttle are infected with buttons, selectors, dials and switches. The cockpit is soundproof, save for the hiss of incoming conditioned air.

Small and Sparse

The Chipmunk's cockpit is small, sparse and smells faintly of oil and petrol. The pilot closes the canopy by sliding it forwards on a rail; it's neither soundproof nor draughtproof. The cockpit can be heated, but the heater's either on or off. The engine sends a soothing vibration through the airframe and you can both hear and feel what it's doing. The control column is literally a pole, with a single radio transmit button on top. The throttle is a simple lever topped by a metal ball.

In the 'Chippy' you feel every bump on the ground and in the air. The difference is visceral, the experience of flying made more real. Typhoon is a detached affair, efficient, easy to fly, but not challenging for the pilot. Every input made on the Chipmunk's controls requires another one or more to keep the aircraft flying accurately. It is a joy to fly and a constant challenge.

By contrast, Typhoon goes where you point it, trims itself out and is immensely easy to fly accurately. Of course, this is as it should be – the Typhoon pilot needs to be concentrating on the tactical situation so that he or she can use the aircraft as a weapon. Flying should not be a distraction, and it isn't. Operating, not flying, is the skill in Typhoon. But this considerably reduces the pilot's sense of satisfaction in the flying.

After 10 hours in the Chippy's front seat I'd gained sufficient experience and the Boss at the time, Squadron Leader Ian 'Smithy' Smith, converted me to the rear seat. The view forward from the Chippy's rear cockpit is restricted, forcing you to use lateral cues when landing. This technique, alien to the modern pilot, is key to landing the Hurricane and Spitfire with their similarly limited view over the nose.

After another 15 hours or so in the Chippy, the next test is to fly a World War Two piston trainer. Many wartime pilots trained on the North American Harvard and today BBMF 'borrows' an aircraft from the warbird community, but when I was doing my training, the RAF had access to a QinetiQ Harvard at Boscombe Down.

So I went flying in a vivid yellow Harvard, along with Dave Southwood, a former RAF fast jet pilot, test pilot and experienced warbird flyer. He taught me to fly from the front seat on the first sortie, with an array of landings on grass and tarmac, with a headwind and with a crosswind. In the afternoon, he sat in the front and we did the same practice with me in the back. It wasn't pretty, but he was sufficiently unshaken to recommend that I progress to the Hurricane.

April Hurricane

There's a day of ground school prior to flying the Hurricane, followed by a briefing on its handling by the Boss. With this complete, »

Now OC BBMF, Milli taxiies in after his first Hurricane sortie on April 2, 2012. SAC Graham Taylor/© UK MoD Crown Copyright 2017

May 2012 and Chipmunk WK518 awaits its next sortie, just a month or so after Millie had graduated onto the Hurricane. Clive Rowley

"As we climbed I finally understood what so many wartime pilots talked about – a crispness and precision of control, a sense of complete communion with the aircraft."

the aircraft was strapped down and I did an engine run to get used to the sound and drills. I couldn't believe I was about to start a Merlin engine. Even as I type the sentence it seems unreal!

With the Merlin running I was surprised not only by how loud it was, but also its tone. From outside it's symphonic, a pitch-perfect engine note. Inside it's very loud indeed and has a different note, neither as sweet nor distinctive. Under Smithy's watchful eye and unable to stop smiling, I ran the engine up a couple of times before shutting down. A few days later I was allowed to taxi her. I took her for a rather ginger spin around the airfield taxiways, with Smithy and his nominated successor as boss, Sqn Ldr Dunc Mason, following in a car, like a duckling following its mother, but somehow the other way around.

Finally, the big day arrived – April 2, 2012 – my first flight in a Hurricane. Smithy gave me a detailed brief on the sortie. As I walked out to the aircraft, I noticed a crowd of people gathered to watch. I did an especially thorough walkaround and patted her on the nose out of sight of the throng, with a gentle word to encourage her to be good to me for my first trip. Then I strapped in. The start was good and after a 'faff' caused by me dropping my checklist, I called for 'taxi' and I was away.

On the runway I advanced the throttle, carefully at first to keep her straight, then up to take-off power, and pushed the control column forward. The tail came up smoothly and after a moment we were airborne. I brought the undercarriage up and waited for the red lights (contrary to modern standards, where red lights are bad news). First the right then the left lights came on and she was 'clean'. Off we went to the north. Holy cow – I was flying a Hurricane!

Even though we were travelling at a quarter of the Typhoon's cruise speed, the noise and unfamiliar environment were slightly disorientating and I was working hard. I had a two-second moment where I looked out along the wing and realised I was actually flying a Hurricane, then it was back to the job at hand, otherwise the aircraft would leave me behind. I stalled her for practice and then ran through the display sequence twice at height. Then we recovered to Coningsby.

This was the really important part – everything else had been a sideshow compared to this – landing. Ordinarily something that didn't even get a thought, now it occupied my mind fully. A plethora of inertial and aerodynamic forces affect the aircraft during touchdown and deceleration. Landing sweetly, on speed, with no lateral movement and then keeping her straight, is key. The boys were in the tower watching like hawks through binoculars.

Smithy had told me to land with the canopy open so I could sit as high as possible. I'd never flown an aircraft with the canopy open before and hadn't given it any real consideration. I pulled the canopy open on its rail... The airflow hit me and the ends of my straps flapped violently and distractingly on my chest. I hadn't expected that!

I selected the gear down and the two green lights quickly illuminated, then I selected the flap. Immediately there was a very pronounced nose down pitch and I went with the aircraft, like someone being pulled along by a large dog on a lead. The speed was very stable and easy to control around finals. I lined up with the runway, had a final quick check of the speed and then we were into the landing.

I started the flare, expecting to land a little later than we did. There was a slight bounce, but we were down! Directional control wasn't too difficult and we come to a halt, turned around, taxied back and set off again. I did two more circuits and then we were done. I taxied her back to dispersal and shut down with immense relief. I was met by the rest of the fighter pilots and Smithy, brandishing a bottle of Champagne. I'd just had the greatest privilege in aviation and joined the small cadre of warbird pilots.

Spitfire Conversion

A few weeks later I'd flown the Hurricane enough for Smithy to convert me to the Spitfire. I was standing beside that divine silver Mk IX. I'd been given the cockpit familiarisation – there are a lot of similarities between the two types and in many regards the Spitfire is actually simpler than the Hurricane. The similarities make this first sortie less daunting, although the elongated nose of the Spitfire completely obscures the forward view on the ground, whereas in the Hurricane you can cheat and peer over the nose if you push yourself up on the pedals. Starting is a little more complicated, but I got her going and we taxied out.

I noticed the take-off attitude is slightly different and then the wheels left the concrete and we were up. The Mk IX's roll rate is similar to the Hurri's (something peculiar to our Mk IX, because the Mk II and V roll very crisply), while the elevators are very light. I'd got more capacity thanks my Hurricane experience, so I looked out along my silver wings and drank in the moment.

As we climbed I finally understood what so many wartime pilots talked about – a crispness and precision of control, a sense of complete communion with the aircraft. We stalled, did a high-speed dive and a couple of display practices. All too soon it was time to go home. Once again there was a fear at the back of my mind; landing a Spitfire is more difficult than landing a Hurricane because the wheels are closer together and the rudder is smaller and less effective.

On my first attempt to land, I over controlled in pitch – my muscle memory was tuned to the Hurricane and the Spitfire is far more sensitive. I overshot and tried again. The next time we made it to the tarmac, although we bounced slightly on touchdown. The next landing was no better, but we kept straight and then we were rolling gently down the runway. We taxied back to the engineers and shut down, relieved. There was no greeting party this time and I walked in alone, casting a wistful and admiring glance back at the Spit, the engine ticking and clicking as it cooled.

And that's how we convert jet fighter pilots to fly our piston fighters. Even now, as OC BBMF, with overall responsibility for fighter pilot training, it all seems too good to be true. It's like one of those fantastically realistic dreams that you believe, even after you wake…

Milli takes a moment to contemplate the occasion in P7's cockpit, after his first flight in the Battle of Britain Spitfire on September 4, 2012. © UK MoD Crown Copyright 2017

Photographed in February 2015, WG486 wears the BBMF badge on its tail. The Chipmunks fly all year round, enabling fighter pilot conversion and currency training. Cpl Phil Major/© UK MoD Crown Copyright 2017

Like all Spitfire Mk XVIs, TE311 was manufactured at Supermarine's Castle Bromwich factory and powered by a Packard Merlin. Completed as a low-backed, clipped-wing Packard Merlin 266-powered LF.Mk XVIE during 1945, the aircraft was delivered to 39 MU at Colerne on June 8, exactly one month after VE-Day.

With the war in Europe over, TE311 was placed in storage until its allocation to the Empire Central Flying School Handling Squadron at Hullavington on October 5, 1945. The unit's role was to assess the handling qualities of all the aircraft types in RAF service and produce authoritative *Pilots' Notes*. TE311 remained on strength until mid-February 1946, when it was delivered to 33 MU at Lyneham, where it was stored for the next five years.

On May 31, 1951, TE311 was placed on charge with No. 1689 Ferry Pilots' Training Flight at RAF Aston Down. Only three weeks later, on June 21, it suffered an accident after its starboard tyre burst on landing. The Spitfire sustained Category 3R damage (repairable on site by a repair organisation). It seems that repairs by a party from Vickers Armstrong took some time, since TE311 did not fly again until December. In July 1952 it was transferred to the Ferry Training Unit at RAF Benson, continuing in the same role until it was returned to 33 MU in September for storage.

Between January 12 and February 23, 1954, TE311 was taken out of storage and loaned to No. 2 Civilian Anti-Aircraft Co-operation Unit at Langham, Norfolk. It is not known in what capacity the unit used the aircraft and it was only at Langham for six weeks, before returning to storage with the MU at Lyneham.

Guarding Tangmere

On December 13, 1954, having flown only 30 hours, TE311 was transferred to non-effective stock, grounded, but still in RAF hands. On August 8, 1955, it was allocated to RAF Tangmere as a gate guardian, for display at the station's main gate. After 12 years of standing outside in the elements, TE311 was loaned to Spitfire Productions Ltd for use in the epic film *Battle of Britain*.

It was restored to taxiing condition and modified with a false high-back rear fuselage, in keeping with Battle of Britain-era Spitfires, for appearances in the film's ground scenes. Its brief spell as a movie extra over, TE311 was returned to its normal configuration and in August 1968 went to guard the gate at RAF Benson, where it spent the next four-and-a half years.

Late in January 1973, TE311 was allocated to the RAF Exhibition Flight based at RAF Bicester and, from 1976, RAF Abingdon. For many years it toured the country by road as a static exhibit, in company with Spitfire Mk XVI TB382. Both were crudely modified for ease of dismantling, loading, transport and reassembly, their wings being regularly removed and refitted.

In 1999, the RAF announced that the two exhibition Mk XVIs were to be put up for disposal. BBMF pointed out that these were RAF aircraft that could be a useful source of spares for the Service's operational Spitfires and after high-level negotiations, TE311 and TB382 were delivered to Coningsby for spares recovery.

TB382 was thus broken up for spares and struck off charge, but BBMF's engineers inspected TE311 and found it in a fairly good state of preservation. While much work was required and many parts were missing, they considered it a candidate for restoration to flight.

Spitfire LF.Mk XVIE TE311

Squadron Leader Clive Rowley MBE RAF (Retd) tells the story of BBMF's Spitfire LF.Mk XVIE TE311

Chief Technician Paul Blackah and his team chose to finish the newly restored TE311 in this carefully researched 74 Sqn scheme. © UK MoD Crown Copyright 2017

Then OC Ops at Coningsby, Wing Commander Paul 'Godders' Godfrey performs a fiery 'hot start' during TE's first PDA session in April 2013. Promoted Group Captain, Godders subsequently became station commander at RAF Lossiemouth. SAC Graham Taylor/© UK MoD Crown Copyright 2017

BBMF engineer Chief Technician Paul Blackah MBE took the lead in the decision and subsequent restoration, aware that it would provide the Flight a sixth airworthy Spitfire of a mark absent from its contemporary fleet, but which had been important in its very early days.

TE311's restoration began in June 2002, initially without official backing or funding, not least because is was supposed to be part of a spares recovery programme. Work was carried out in the volunteer team's own time, over lunch breaks, after the working day had ended and at weekends, but eventually it was agreed that the TE311 would officially be placed on BBMF strength.

It flew again for the first time in more than 58 years on Friday, October 19, 2012, in the capable hands of Sqn Ldr Ian Smith MBE, then OC BBMF. Not surprisingly, there were teething problems to iron out, but TE311 was ready and available to play a full part in the 2013 display season. Since then it has become a Flight stalwart and favourite among the BBMF fighter pilots.

2017 Scheme

For the 2017 season, TE represents Spitfire Mk XVI TD240/SZ-G, the personal aircraft of Gp Capt Aleksander Gabszewicz, commanding No. 131 (Polish) Wing during the closing stages of the war in Europe in 1945. This aircraft sported Gabszewicz's personal emblem of a boxing bulldog on the port engine cowling. The 'SZ' code letters were Gabszewicz's personal choice, not actually representing an aircraft of 316 (Polish) Squadron, but showing his affection for the unit he had previously commanded, combined with his initial 'G'.

When TD240 was delivered to 131 Wing on April 20, 1945, it was based at B.101 Nordhorn in Germany, but shortly afterwards moved to B.113 Varrelbusch. Gabszewicz flew six operational sorties in it, including four dive-bombing missions. By the end of the war his score was 9½ enemy aircraft confirmed destroyed in air combat (including 3 shared 'halves'), 1½ probably destroyed and 2 damaged.

Gabszewicz was decorated with the Gold and Silver Cross of the Order of Virtuti Militari, Polish Cross of Valour and three Bars, DSO and Bar, DFC and the French Croix de Guerre with Palm. He died in 1983 and in 1992 his ashes were dropped over Warsaw and Dęblin, where he had trained and where he scored his initial victory of the war on the first day of conflict, September 1, 1939.

Group Captain Aleksander Gabszewicz poses with a Spitfire in October 1944. Via BBMF

The striking nose art on Gabszewicz's Spitfire XVI TD240. Via BBMF

The first time I ever flew a Spitfire, I flew MK356. For that reason alone she will always hold a special place in my heart, like the first person you fell in love with. But there's a far more important reason for MK being special on BBMF, because we use her and Mk XVI TE311 to convert our pilots from the Hurricane to the Spitfire.

MK and TE are different to the 'baby' Spits (Mk IIA and VB), featuring several subtle but important improvements over those earlier marks. Firstly, and most importantly when converting BBMF pilots, they have a taller, wider 'broad chord' rudder. This significantly improves directional control, making the aircraft more manageable on landing, especially with a crosswind.

The Spitfire was designed to operate from grass aerodromes on which it could always be landed into wind. Modern airfields have hard runways that are often affected by crosswinds, which adds to the challenge of landing a Spitfire and keeping it straight. All aircraft have a crosswind limit, the magnitude of the crosswind component above which the controls of the aircraft run out of authority, and for the Spitfire we have very strict crosswind limits.

Monroe?

Secondly and almost as importantly, MK and TE are heavier than the babies. That's not to say they're overweight, but perhaps more Marilyn Monroe compared to Audrey Hepburn. It means they're more willing to 'sit' on the runway during landing, while the Mk II and V are desperate to continue flying when you want them to land. Trying to land even 5kt fast in a baby Spitfire will result in the aircraft floating a considerable distance or, worse still, one wing lifting if conditions are at all gusty.

Thirdly, the undercarriage is raked forward slightly and the wheels a little larger on the later marks, helping reduce the babies' 'skittishness' on the ground. Thus the Mk IX and XVI enable pilots to gain experience and confidence on the Spitfire before they're exposed to the earlier marks.

Quite apart from these practicalities, it's impossible to forget when you fly MK356 that you're flying a Spitfire with an impressive wartime pedigree of 60 missions in 60 days, one that was hit by enemy ground fire three times and which delivered air support to the D-Day landings in June 1944!

Flying MK

Squadron Leader Andy 'Milli' Millikin recalls his first flight in BBMF's Spitfire Mk IX and explains its operational importance

MK was wearing this spectacular silver scheme when Milli first made its acquaintance. Paul E Eden

BBMF's Operations Officer, Flight Lieutenant Antony 'Parky' Parkinson MBE, recalls the first time he flew Spitfire XVIE TE311

It was a typically blustery, late September Sunday in 2012 when I pulled the fuel cut-off lever rearwards for the last time in Spitfire Mk XIX PM631, signalling the end of another busy BBMF summer season. As the five-bladed propeller ground to a halt, I felt the usual tinge of sadness that I wouldn't have the privilege of flying one of these wonderfully iconic aircraft for another six months. Even the faded gold autumnal leaves drifting down nearby seemed to reflect my mood. Or maybe not…

The Boss, Squadron Leader Dunc Mason, had mentioned that the latest addition to the hangar – Spitfire Mk XVI TE311, which I'd seen slowly taking shape over the last decade – would require a few shakedown sorties over the winter. Quite surprisingly (and without any coercion required) he had agreed that it would be beneficial for another pilot – me – to fly her. Genius! I was in!

With pride and a whiff of envy, I'd watched as former Boss 'Smithy' and new Boss Dunc flew the new Spit. I observed them linger a little longer than usual post shut down, not wanting to leave the cockpit. Flying any 'new' Spitfire for the first time is incredibly special, but they both seemed more moved by the event than I'd expected. I listened intently as they answered the obvious question, "What's she like to fly?" I remember phrases like 'utterly beautiful' and 'bloody brilliant' in reply. Now it was my turn.

December Day

December 6 was a beautiful clear winter's day. 'TE' glinted resplendently in the low sun and waited patiently for me to strap in and perform my checks. I imagined she was as keen as I was to be off, once again back up where she belonged after her 58-year lay-off. I had already ground run her and given her a taxi check, but yet again I was amazed how smoothly her Merlin 266 engine ran.

TE's bubble canopy and cut-down rear fuselage give the aircraft a unique look among the Flight's Spitfires. The configuration also makes for a very different view from the cockpit. SAC Jack Welson/© UK MoD Crown Copyright 2017

TE311's propeller begins to turn as the Merlin 266 smokes into life, late in the 2013 season.
Sgt Peter George/© UK MoD Crown Copyright 2017

"I reckon you've built the best handling Spitfire in the world!"

The view out front was much the same as from other Spits, that long nose pointing up at the sky and impairing forward vision, but it was so different looking sideways and rearwards. The clipped wings seemed ridiculously short from the cockpit and even with the bubble canopy closed, the view from the low-back cockpit was spectacular for 'checking six'. The ratchet handle on the right-hand side for closing the canopy was instinctive to operate and then I was cocooned in the beautifully detailed cockpit, waiting for her to warm up.

As the oil temperature crept up to 40°C, I completed my power checks and lined up on the runway. I often find myself subconsciously talking to these beautiful pieces of machinery; it was no different now. Power coming up smoothly, blending in right rudder, checking 3,000rpm, +4 on the boost and easing the stick forward. Tail's up nice and quickly and she's as straight as a die; 80kt and pull her off the ground. Squeeze the brakes on and off and gear up. UP/UP red lights lit. Happy days. Throttle back to 2,400rpm and up into the blue we go.

Dunc had briefed me to take her up to around 5,000ft and perform a couple of stalls in the clean and dirty (gear and flaps down) configurations to get the of feel her, before flying some aerobatics in the overhead for 10 minutes, then popping her back down. As she'd had a complete rebuild and such a long stint on the ground, manoeuvring her up to +3*g* would perhaps reveal any 'gremlins'. The best place to be was in the overhead of the airfield; if anything untoward happened with the engine I would have »

TE flew its first display season in 2013. Here Parky, in the cockpit, and 'Godders' Godfrey catch up during the year's PDA session. Sgt Mobbs/© UK MoD Crown Copyright 2017

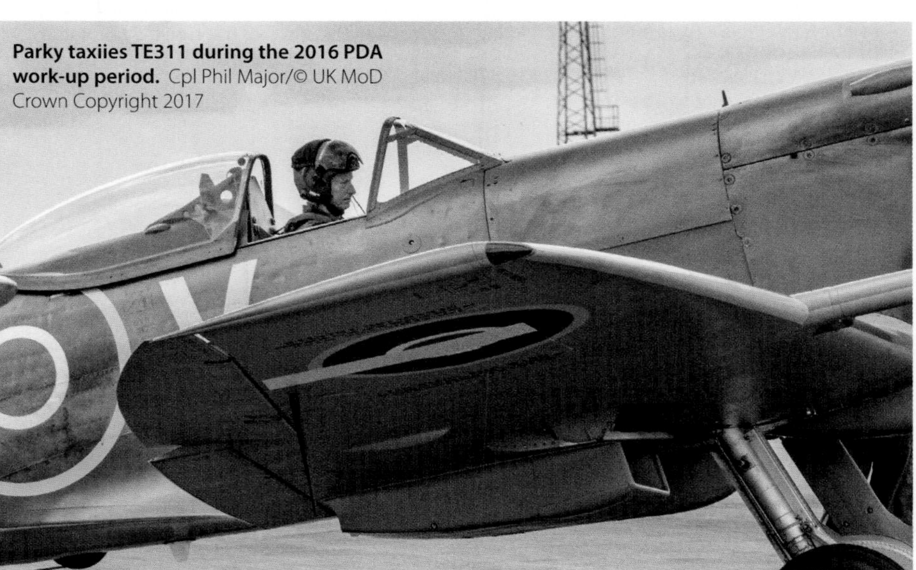
Parky taxiies TE311 during the 2016 PDA work-up period. Cpl Phil Major/© UK MoD Crown Copyright 2017

the height and energy to glide her back to Coningsby's main runway.

Prior to stalling I couldn't resist seeing how she rolled. I'd flown our Mk IX Spit when she'd had clipped wings, but I couldn't really notice the improved roll rate that clipping the wings was intended to generate. This was different. Stick fully left with a blend of left rudder and... wow, spectacular! Now to the right (against the torque from the powerful four-bladed propeller) and again, noticeably quicker.

Time for the stalls and she exhibited the usual benign Spitfire characteristics, a reluctance to stop flying even when the airspeed is deliberately bled to below 50kt. Heavy buffet, but no wing drop, and instant recovery when the control column is moved forwards to unstall the wings and power is applied. Wartime fighter pilots must have loved these forgiving qualities when they took their Spitfires to the edge of the flying envelope (and often beyond) in combat.

TE was officially unveiled to the world on December 13, 2012. Paul E Eden

"I'd watched as former Boss 'Smithy' and new Boss Dunc flew the new Spit."

Power On, Nose Down

Now for some aeros. We're lined up with the runway, power on, nose down. The speed rapidly builds to 250kt and I gently ease straight back on the stick. Squint at the G meter, a little over +3*g*, initially easing in right rudder during the pull, then blending in left rudder as she slows inverted at the top of the loop. Gyroscopic effect, then torque from the mighty Merlin do their bit on the Spitfire's airframe. Head back (no mirror on this Spit) to keep her straight and I'm picking up the line of the runway below. There's no buffet and just light inputs on the stick pull her out of the ensuing dive. Fantastic. Might as well go straight into another one... The next 10 minutes passed by in a blur, 'TE' and myself enjoying seeing the world revolve around us.

Inevitably it came time to land. The engine temperatures and pressures were all normal, so I positioned for a 'hangar break' – throttle back to cruise power and let the speed build for a low pass over the BBMF hangar; 240kt, that's nice and fast for the power setting, and a climbing turn to downwind.

Throttle back and pop the radiator flaps open. With the speed bleeding back to 150kt, I wind the canopy handle backwards to get the bubble canopy open. It's much easier than on the other Spits and there's no need to swap hands to lock the canopy with the door. I smoothly select fine pitch, and at 100kt swap hands to select the gear down. A nice slow cadence and the reassuring 'clunk, clunk' as the gear locks thump into place. Green lights (gear locked down indicators) lit, so I select the flap lever down. I feel the drag as the flaps bite and take a quick glance left and right to see both flap-down indicators had popped up on the wings. I turn finals and trim her out, then squeeze the brakes on and off to check the brake pressures. All good. She was ready to land.

Breathe Again

The speed falls back to just under 90kt with a trickle of power; that's OK. Concentration is now between the airspeed and runway picture. Rolling out on finals, that long nose obscures the view out front again. Speed just above 80kt. There's no real crosswind to contend with today and I'm aware of the ground getting closer as the sides of the runway come into my peripheral vision. I gently arrest the rate of descent, but keep her coming down. Going to touch soon, so I gently throttle back to idle. The propeller rotation seems so slow. Then stick still further back and we gently touch down.

She's lovely and straight. Phew! Let the tailwheel drop the last few inches. The nose rises still further and then smoothly fully back on the stick to hold the tail down. Concentrate now. This is where a Spit often darts off line – maybe to the right, but could be left – as the various tail-dragger landing nuances are magnified by its narrow-track undercarriage. But nothing. Only tiny rudder inputs are required to keep her straight. Time to breathe again.

Taxi in and shut down. Helmet off. No rush. Think I'll linger here just a little bit longer than usual...

After I signed her in, I had one last job to do. Chief Tech Paul Blackah, who led the rebuild of this magnificent Spitfire, was away. So I sent him a quick text message: "I reckon you've built the best handling Spitfire in the world!". ⊙

The clipped wings make a very obvious difference to the classic Spitfire shape. Pilots note a dramatic increase in roll rate. © UK MoD Crown Copyright 2017

Hurricane Mk IIC PZ865

Squadron Leader Clive Rowley MBE RAF (Retd) tells the story of BBMF's Hurricane Mk IIC PZ865

Hurricane Mk IIC PZ865 was the last Hurricane built from a total of 14,533. Fitted with four 20mm cannon and a Rolls-Royce Merlin XX engine, it came off the Hawker production line at Langley on July 27, 1944, with the inscription 'The Last of the Many' painted beneath the cockpit on both sides.

George Bulman, who had piloted the maiden flight of the prototype Hurricane in 1935, test flew PZ865 later that day, therefore completing the initial flights of the first and last Hurricanes.

Hawker purchased PZ865 back from the Air Ministry so that it could be preserved for posterity. In 1950, wearing the civilian registration G-AMAU and a smart Oxford blue and gold colour scheme, PZ865 was entered in the King's Cup Air Race, sponsored by HRH Princess Margaret. Flown by Group Captain Peter Townsend CVO DSO DFC and Bar, it achieved second place. Over the next three years the aircraft participated in several other air races, being modified for racing with the removal of its cannon and the installation of two 'overload' wing fuel tanks.

Subsequently, PZ865 flew in various capacities under Hawker Siddeley ownership. By the 1960s, it had been returned to its original camouflage scheme and become part of an unofficial collection of historic Hawker aircraft, including a 1924 Hawker Cygnet, a Hart and a Sea Fury, all based at the company's Dunsfold airfield. The Hurricane made numerous appearances at air displays in the hands of company test pilots, including Bill Bedford OBE AFC and Duncan Simpson OBE. It was also flown for films, including *Battle of Britain*.

PZ865 emerged from deep maintenance in 2012 painted to represent 34 Sqn Hurricane Mk IIC HW840/EG-S, flown by Canadian Flt Lt Jimmy Whalen DFC, with South East Asia Command in 1944. Cpl Phil Major/© UK MoD Crown Copyright 2017

"It's a Hurricane, flight sergeant, a very special Hurricane, and I'm handing it over to you."
Duncan Simpson, Hawker Siddeley Chief Test Pilot

Before taking its current scheme, PZ represented Mk IIC 'JX-E', flown by 1 Sqn's Flt Lt Karel Kuttelwascher DFC. The Czech pilot flew 'JX-E', named *NIGHT REAPER*, with considerable success on night intruder operations over occupied Europe. Paul E Eden

PZ865 wore its 'The Last of the Many' inscription into its BBMF ownership. Key Collection

Above: PZ865 was the last Hurricane off the production line. Key Collection

BBMF Hurricane

In 1971, having been grounded for a while, PZ865 was fully refurbished to flying condition. In 1972, a combination of limited resources and restricted hangar space at Dunsfold led Hawker Siddeley to decide that it could no longer maintain its historic aircraft collection. Suddenly, Hurricane PZ865's future as a 'flyer' was very uncertain, but the intervention of Duncan Simpson, now Hawker Siddeley Chief Test Pilot, and some astute manoeuvring behind the scenes, resulted in the Hurricane's donation to the BBMF at RAF Coltishall.

In March 1972, before anyone could change their mind, Duncan Simpson delivered PZ865 to the Norfolk station. His arrival with this precious piece of British aviation history was unexpected. A BBMF flight sergeant greeted him: "Afternoon sir, what have we here?" Duncan replied, "It's a Hurricane, flight sergeant, a very special Hurricane, and I'm handing it over to you. Look after it and make sure it's flying right into the future so that future generations can see it."

For many years the aircraft appeared with the BBMF as 'The Last of the Many', but eventually the fabric bearing the inscription was removed and placed on display at BBMF headquarters. The Lincolnshire Lancaster Association funded replica 20mm cannon, which were fitted to PZ865 in 1996, restoring its appearance to that of a Hurricane Mk IIC.

As G-AMAU, PZ865 flew as an air racer long before joining BBMF. Key Collection

Chipmunk Cherished

The Royal Air Force replaced one classic elementary trainer, the de Havilland Tiger Moth, with another, the de Havilland Canada Chipmunk

Primarily a manufacturer of light aircraft, during the 1920s the de Havilland company gained considerable success with its Moth series of sporting and touring biplanes. Such was the aircrafts' popularity that de Havilland created a Canadian subsidiary in Toronto, specifically to build Moths for the local market. Its output soon included the Tiger Moth, which became the mainstay of Royal Air Force elementary flying training from 1932 until the late 1940s.

Known as de Havilland Canada, the company later took a major role in wartime Mosquito production, but as peace became likely, thoughts turned to creating its own line of aircraft, independent of the UK parent.

First among these was the DHC-1 Chipmunk, an elementary trainer very much in the mould of the ubiquitous Tiger Moth, but with a modern monoplane configuration and enclosed cockpit. The type first flew on May 22, 1946 and 158 were built for the Royal Canadian Air Force and other customers, before Toronto production ceased in 1951.

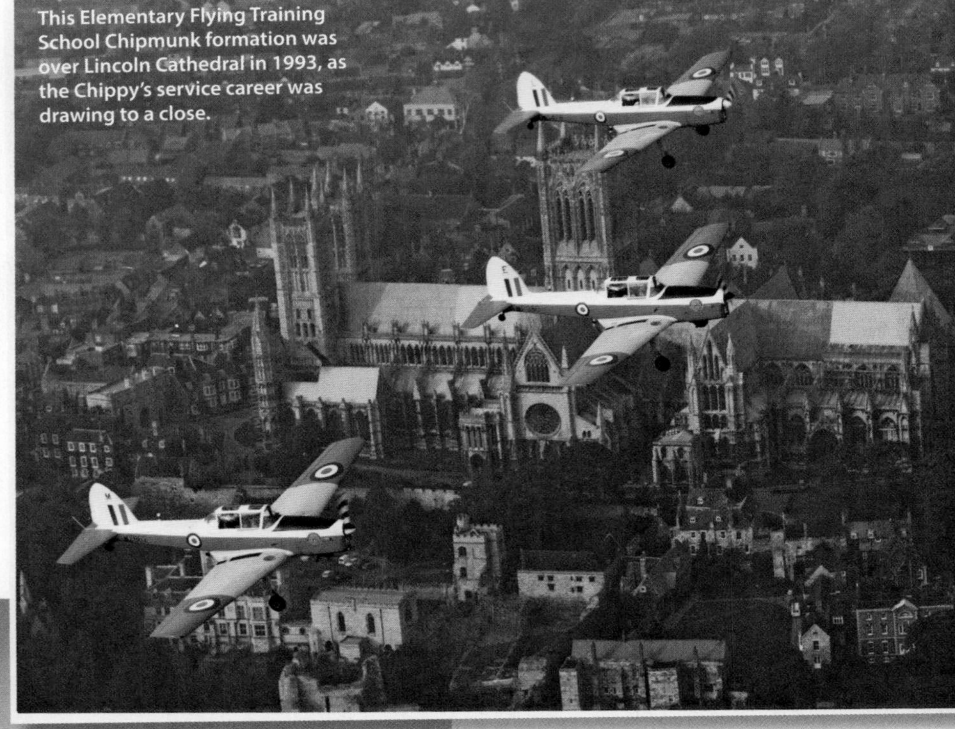

This Elementary Flying Training School Chipmunk formation was over Lincoln Cathedral in 1993, as the Chippy's service career was drawing to a close.

WB555 was among the first ten Chippys off the de Havilland line. This early image shows it in the silver scheme, with yellow 'trainer' bands. All Key Collection unless stated otherwise

British Chippy

In an ironic twist of fate, the RAF evaluated the de Havilland Canada product at Boscombe Down and found it an ideal Tiger Moth replacement. Its conclusion was largely based on a civilian-registered aircraft equipped with blind flying panels, a radio and variable-pitch propeller, all to RAF specifications. Production for UK use was assigned to de Havilland.

The work was completed very quickly – 740 Chipmunk T.Mk 10 aircraft had been delivered by the time the last arrived on October 1, 1953 and the universally accepted nickname 'Chippy' was soon applied. The type began replacing the Tiger Moth with Oxford University Air Squadron (UAS) in 1950 and soon became common with UASs around the country, as well as the Reserve Flying Schools, Royal Air Force College Cranwell and as an ab initio trainer for National Service pilots.

Communications work also came the Chippy's way while in July 1965, the Primary Flying Squadron at South Cerney began using it as the first step for students destined to complete their initial jet training on the Hunting Percival Jet Provost. In 1973, the more capable Scottish Aviation Bulldog began replacing the Chipmunk in the primary

This was the original de Havilland Canada Chipmunk prototype.

The British Army and Royal Navy, as here, were also Chipmunk operators.

training role, releasing more of the veteran Chippys for the Air Experience Flights (AEFs) providing Air Cadets with their first taste of flying.

In an unusual 38-year extension of its communications task, the Chippy's role out of Gatow, Berlin saw the front-seater equipped with a camera, these Chipmunk 'spyplanes' gathering photographic intelligence as they exercised the UK's right to fly in designated sectors around the isolated city.

Gatow relinquished WG466 and WG486, its final Chippy pair, in 1994. The latter eventually found its way to Coningsby, where it remains in BBMF service. The Chippy continued in limited AEF use until 1996, bringing to a close 45 years of faithful service, albeit that two aircraft remain as indispensable BBMF fighter pilot training aids. ⊙

WK518's open cowling panels reveal something of its de Havilland Gipsy Major 8 piston engine. Its predecessor, the Tiger Moth employed a lower powered Gipsy Major. Cpl Phil Major/© UK MoD Crown Copyright 2017

PZ865 launches for an evening training sortie on August 13, 2014, during the two Lancasters work-up period. © Paul E Eden

"While considered easier to land than the Spitfire, the Hurricane still offers considerable challenges to a pilot new to warbirds."

Flying PZ

PZ865 taxies to Coningsby's runway. LAC Megan Woodhouse/© UK MoD Crown Copyright 2017

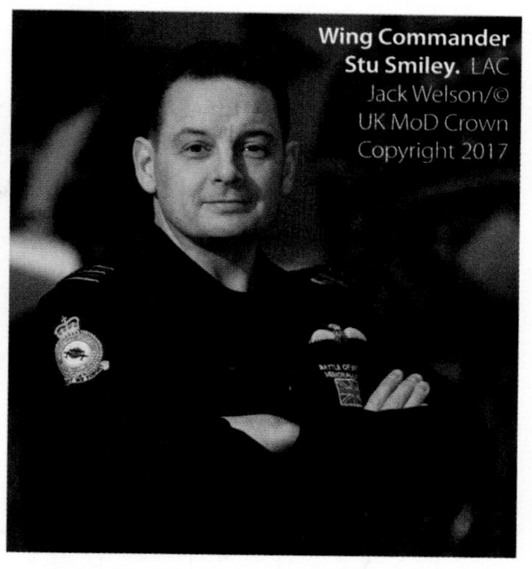

Wing Commander Stu Smiley. LAC Jack Welson/© UK MoD Crown Copyright 2017

Wing Commander Stu Smiley shares the experience of flying Hurricane PZ865

As a new fighter pilot on the RAF BBMF, you're introduced to the fighters via the Hurricane. In 2016, I flew my first solo on type, on Mk IIC PZ865.

It is said that as a pilot you never forget your first solo and this is very true. I clearly remember the fear, trepidation and underlying excitement of my first time in the Chipmunk, as a young and inexperienced student.

Twenty-six years later, flying PZ865, those feelings were re-ignited and magnified beyond all expectation. It's difficult to express in words the immense privilege and honour that comes with flying the BBMF aircraft – perhaps the fear and trepidation is easier to relate!

The moment you strap in to her beautifully maintained cockpit, the reality of what you're about to do comes into stark focus. The Hurricane is a large aircraft, significantly more so than the Spitfire, and you feel this on the ground as much as you do when you first take to the air. The power, heat and noise from the Rolls-Royce Merlin are breathtaking and you take solace in the fact that all those outside the cockpit hear is the rhythmic purr of a perfect engine.

First Take-off

That first take-off roll, in an unfamiliar cockpit, with the almost overwhelming sensory inputs from the engine, creates an environment like no other. Airborne for the first time, you experience the mushy controls and what becomes a familiar dead spot, and you're almost convinced that perhaps this aircraft should not be flying.

But that very quickly changes. From the moment of initial climb out, with the gear retracted and all engine indications normal, the realisation of what you're doing begins to dawn. You're in a Hurricane, a flying legend! The huge respect you had for those World War Two veterans has just grown immensely.

At normal cruise speeds PZ is a delight to fly; she's smooth and responsive, her controls perfectly balanced. The iconic external purr of the Merlin is a distinctly angry growl from within, serving as a useful reminder that she's not to be trifled with.

In the BBMF display sequence, PZ is best flown two-handed, for at high speed the controls become very heavy. However, at these speeds she's rock steady and it's easy to see why the Hurricane was considered such a stable gun platform in air-to-air combat.

While considered easier to land than the Spitfire, the Hurricane still offers considerable challenges to a pilot new to warbirds. The view over the nose is reasonable for a tail-dragger but, even applying all the techniques we're meticulously trained in, the result on touchdown can be emotional! It's certainly fair to say that the elation of my first flight in PZ was not truly felt until I'd landed her safely back at Coningsby, taxied in without incident and shut down. ⊙

Chipmunk T.Mk 10 WG486 & WK518

Squadron Leader Clive Rowley MBE RAF (Retd) tells the story of BBMF's Chipmunk T.Mk 10s WG486 and WK518

The two de Havilland Canada Chipmunks held on BBMF charge are the last in RAF service and the least seen of the Flight's aircraft. Used year round, they are primarily for the conversion and continuation training of BBMF fighter pilots on tailwheel aircraft, but also fly reconnaissance of new venues, drop-off or collect pilots and, occasionally, deliver small spare parts.

WG486

Chipmunk T10 WG486 was built in the de Havilland factory on Hawarden airfield at Broughton, near Chester, the same facility where Lancaster PA474 was manufactured in 1945.

WG486 was delivered to the RAF in January 1952 and served with No. 5 Basic Flying Training School, No. 9 Refresher Flying School and No. 2 Flying Training School (FTS), before being used by Nos 651 and 657 Squadrons, Army Air Corps.

In December 1958 it was issued to 114 Sqn on Cyprus, where it was used in operations against Ethniki Organosis Kyprion Agoniston (EOKA, The National Union of Cypriot Combatants), flying low-level reconnaissance patrols and convoy escort missions from Famagusta, Xeros and Akrotiri airfields, with British Army officers in the rear seat. The crisis ended in March 1959 and WG486 returned to the UK in 1961.

Over the next 16 years it served as a flying trainer with units including the RAF College at Cranwell; Initial Training School at South Cerney and Church Fenton; No. 1 FTS at Linton-on-Ouse; Liverpool and Bristol University Air Squadrons (UASs); and No. 3 Air Experience Flight (AEF) at Bristol Filton.

In 1987, WG486 was sent to Germany for service with the Gatow Station Flight in West Berlin, which was then surrounded by Soviet Bloc territory, for a second phase of operational flying. For the next two years the Chipmunk was flown on highly secret photographic 'spying' flights in the zone around Berlin.

After RAF Gatow closed, the aircraft spent a year at RAF Laarbruch in Germany, before joining the BBMF in 1995.

WK518

Also built at Hawarden and delivered to the RAF in January 1952, Chipmunk T10 WK518 has been with the BBMF longer than WG486 and always served as a trainer. Its initial service was with the RAF College at Cranwell, where it flew as an elementary trainer, but it also flew with the Liverpool, Manchester, Cambridge, Hull, Leeds and London Universities UASs.

Chipmunk WK518 was delivered to the BBMF from No. 1 Air Experience Flight at Manston, in April 1983.

Above: WG486 wears a scheme similar to that worn by the RAF's current Hawk T2 and Tucano trainers. Key Collection

Chipmunk WK518 is marked 'FLT LT PARKINSON' under its forward cockpit, apparently singling it out as Parky's personal aircraft. In reality it joins WG486 as a workhorse of BBMF fighter pilot training. Cpl Phil Major/© UK MoD Crown Copyright 2017

PS emerged from refurbishment in 2016 wearing a scheme representing 81 Sqn's PS852, a PR.Mk 19 detached to RAF Kai Tak, Hong Kong, in the early 1950s and flown by Flt Lt Edward 'Ted' Powles AFC. SAC Jack Welson/© UK MoD Crown Copyright 2017

Spitfire PR.Mk XIX PM631 & PS915

Squadron Leader Clive Rowley MBE RAF (Retd) tells the story of BBMF's Spitfire PR.Mk XIXs, PM631 and PS915

Spitfire PM631 is thought to have been built at Reading in spring 1944, as a 'production prototype' of the high-altitude photographic-reconnaissance PR.Mk XIX, fitted with a Rolls-Royce Griffon 66 engine and pressurised cockpit. It was delivered to Southampton in May 1944, where Supermarine appears to have used it for PR.Mk XIX component testing.

By March 1946, PM631 was at Benson, the RAF's hub of PR operations. Here it remained until issued to No. 203 Advanced Flying School in May 1949. From June 1950 to June 1951 PM631 was stored with 9 MU at Cosford, except for three weeks' service with 541 Sqn, in Germany, early in 1951.

After modifications for meteorological work, PM631 was leased to Short Brothers from July 2, 1951. Based at Hooton Park on the Wirral peninsula, and then at Woodvale, near Southport, Lancashire, it was flown by the Temperature and Humidity Monitoring (THUM) Flight's civilian pilots. THUM aircraft made daily ascents to 30,000ft to gather meteorological information.

On July 11, 1957, Group Captain Jamie Rankin, DSO and Bar, DFC and Bar, flew PM631 from Duxford to Biggin Hill in formation with ex-THUM Mk XIXs PS853 and PS915 as the founding equipment of the Historic Aircraft Flight, forerunner to the BBMF.

PS915

Built at Southampton (Eastleigh) in 1945, PR.Mk XIX PS915 was delivered to 6 MU at Brize Norton on April 17, 1945. It was transferred to Benson on April 27 and held there until its allocation to 541 Sqn on June 21, 1945. In July 1946, PS915 was moved to the Photographic Reconnaissance Development Unit, also at Benson, for tests with new cameras.

On October 10, 1946 it was allocated to RAF Luneberg, Germany, before joining 2 Sqn at Wunstorf in April 1947. Coded 'OI-K', PS915 served the unit for four years, flying strategic reconnaissance sorties in connection with the East/West divide of Europe and during the politically tense period of the 1948-49 Berlin Airlift.

PS915 returned to the UK in 1951 and, after a period in storage at Cosford and modifications, joined the THUM Flight at Woodvale in June 1954. The Historic Aircraft Flight was inaugurated on July 11, 1957, with PS915 as a founder member – Wing Commander (later Group Captain) Peter Thompson DFC flew it to Biggin Hill from Duxford for the occasion. However, it was in poor shape and soon grounded for many years' service as a gate guardian at various RAF stations.

In June 1984, PS915 was transported to the British Aerospace facility at Samlesbury for a full refurbishment to flying condition. The work included replacing the original Rolls-Royce Griffon 66 with an ex-Shackleton Griffon 58, benefitting from its more readily available spares; the Griffon 58 is now the standard BBMF PR.Mk XIX engine. PS915 joined BBMF in March 1987.

PM has remained on strength through the various unit iterations that led to today's BBMF. Key Collection

Squadrons Then and Now

Number	Established	Initial aircraft	PR.Mk XIX service	2017 Role	Aircraft
2 (II)	May 13, 1912	B.E. prototype & B.E.2	November 1945-March 1951	Air Defence & Offensive Support	Typhoon

The Royal Air Force Battle of Britain Memorial Flight Anniversary Team

With PA474 as backdrop, this photograph represents the team that keeps BBMF in the air, including its many part-time volunteers. Squadron Leader Clive Rowley MBE RAF (Retd) explains who's who

Technicians

The majority of BBMF's technicians are seated on the wings of Hurricane LF363 (at left) and Spitfire P7350. The engineering team comprises 30 full-time RAF personnel.

Public Relations Team

Standing immediately in front of the Lancaster is the 'PR Team', a group of enthusiastic volunteers with other primary roles in the RAF, who travel to airshows and events throughout the display season as BBMF's public face. Their commitment and the call on their personal time is extraordinary. Without their efforts, the Flight would have no ground presence at most events.

Aircrew

Standing in front of the PR Team are the aircrew who fly BBMF's historic aircraft. They are all part-time volunteers with other primary RAF duties, just as it has been since the Flight's formation in 1957. For them, flying the aircraft is a privilege, but also a considerable personal commitment.

The Spitfire and Hurricane pilots have backgrounds as RAF fast-jet pilots. The Dakota and Lancaster are flown by RAF pilots with experience on heavy, multi-engine, multi-crew aircraft, among them the BBMF's volunteer navigators, flight engineers and air loadmasters, who are essential to their safe and efficient operation.

Support Staff

In front of the aircrew is the administration and operations staff. This 'back room' team has been expanded in recent years but is still small, with a very high workload all year round. A serving flight lieutenant – the 'BBMF Chief of Staff' – oversees all administration and PR activities, with a team of PR Officer, Admin Officer and Admin Assistant, all of them civil servants.

An Operations Assistant works with BBMF's Operations Officer, delivering all the necessary support to the Flight's flying activities. Also in the line-up is the Flight's resident 'stores' lady, who works at the BBMF end of the logistics and supply chain.

Management Team

The BBMF Engineering Management Team, near the front, comprises the Flight's Engineering Officer, Warrant Officer Kev Ball; Flight Sergeant 'Deano' McAllister; and Chief Technician Paul Blackah MBE, BBMF Engineering Controller. In their midst is Flight Lieutenant Antony 'Parky' Parkinson MBE, BBMF Operations Officer, who also flies the Spitfires and Hurricanes as one of the Flight's two full-time pilots – the other is OC BBMF.

Flanking them are Wing Commander Stu Smiley (at left), Officer Commanding Operations Wing, RAF Coningsby, who is the BBMF's senior supervisor and also flies the fighters. On the right is another of the fighter pilots, RAF Coningsby's Station Commander – Group Captain Jezz Attridge OBE was in post when the photo was taken, but Group Captain Mike Baulkwill has since replaced him.

Finally, at the very front is Officer Commanding the Royal Air Force Battle of Britain Memorial Flight, Squadron Leader Andy 'Milli' Millikin.